Imperialism
A History in Documents

TROIS COULEURS
UN DRAPEAU
UN EMPIRE

Imperialism
A History in Documents

Bonnie G. Smith

OXFORD
UNIVERSITY PRESS

OXFORD
UNIVERSITY PRESS

Oxford New York

Athens Auckland Bangkok Bogotá Buenos Aries Calcutta Cape Town
Chennai Dar es Salaam Delhi Florence Hong Kong Istanbul Karachi
Kuala Lumpur Madrid Melbourne Mexico City Mumbai Nairobi
Paris São Paulo Singapore Taipei Tokyo Toronto Warsaw

and associated companies in
Berlin Ibadan

Copyright © 2000 by Bonnie G. Smith

Design: Sandy Kaufman
Layout: Loraine Machlin

Published by Oxford University Press, Inc.,
198 Madison Avenue, New York, New York 10016
www.oup.com

Library of Congress Cataloging-in-Publication Data
Smith, Bonnie.
Imperialism: a history in documents / Bonnie Smith.
p. cm. — (Pages from history)
Includes bibliographical references and index.
ISBN 0-19-510801-9 (library binding)
1. Imperialism—History. [1. Imperialism—History—Sources.]
I. Title. II. Series.
JC359.S775 2000
325'.32—dc21
00-028552

1 3 5 7 9 8 6 4 2

Printed in the United States of America
on acid-free paper

Cover: The Colours and Colour Party of
the King's African Rifles, 1914–18.

Frontispiece: "Three colors, one flag, one
empire" reads this French advertisement
between World Wars I and II. Europeans
liked to think that their empires were
models of harmony and unity, despite
tensions, rebellions, and resistance from
their colonial subjects.

Title page: The Empress Dowager Tz'u-hsi
indirectly ruled China from 1865 until
1908, while the forces of European and
Japanese imperialism chipped away at
Chinese independence. An anti-Westerner,
the empress nonetheless posed with the
wives of foreign diplomats early in the
20th century when little remained of
Chinese sovereignty.

Contents

What Is a Document?

To the historian, a document is, quite simply, any sort of historical evidence. It is a primary source, the raw material of history. A document may be more than the expected government paperwork, such as a treaty or passport. It is also a letter, diary, will, grocery list, newspaper article, recipe, memoir, oral history, school yearbook, map, chart, architectural plan, poster, musical score, play script, novel, political cartoon, painting, photograph—even an object.

Using primary sources allows us not just to read *about* history, but to read history itself. It allows us to immerse ourselves in the look and feel of an era gone by, to understand its people and their language, whether verbal or visual. And it allows us to take an active, hands-on role in (re)constructing history.

Using primary sources requires us to use our powers of detection to ferret out the relevant facts and to draw conclusions from them; just as Agatha Christie uses the scores in a bridge game to determine the identity of a murderer, the historian uses facts from a variety of sources—some, perhaps, seemingly inconsequential—to build a historical case.

The poet W. H. Auden wrote that history was the study of questions. Primary sources force us to ask questions—and then, by answering them, to construct a narrative or an argument that makes sense to us. Moreover, as we draw on the many sources from "the dust-bin of history," we can endow that narrative with character, personality, and texture—all the elements that make history so endlessly intriguing.

Cartoon
This political cartoon addresses the issue of church and state. It illustrates the Supreme Court's role in balancing the demands of the First Amendment of the Constitution and the desires of the religious population.

Illustration
Illustrations from children's books, such as this alphabet from the New England Primer, tell us how children were educated, and also what the religious and moral values of the time were.

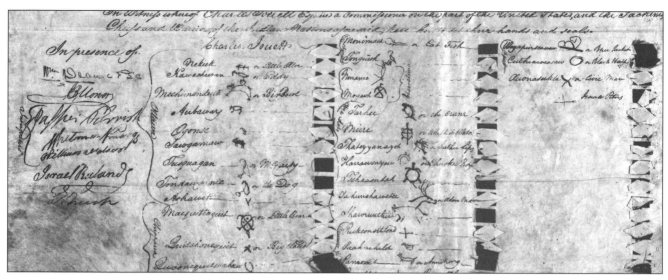

Treaty

A government document such as this 1805 treaty can reveal not only the details of government policy, but information about the people who signed it. Here, the Indians' names were written in English transliteration by U.S. officials; the Indians added pictographs to the right of their names.

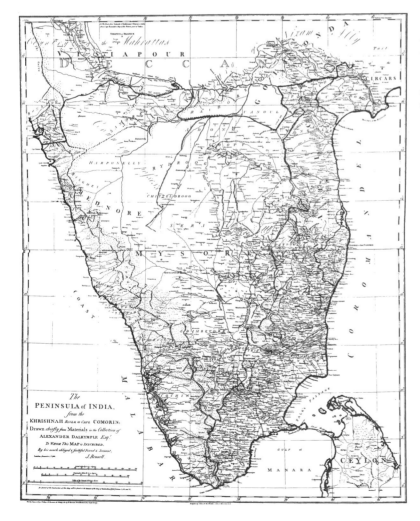

Map

A 1788 British map of India shows the region prior to British colonization, an indication of the kingdoms and provinces whose ethnic divisions would resurface later in India's history.

Literature

The first written version of the Old English epic Beowulf, from the late 10th century, is physical evidence of the transition from oral to written history. Charred by fire, it is also a physical record of the wear and tear of history.

How to Read a Document

The documents in this book come from many parts of the globe and feature the experience of imperialism from the 1870s to the 1930s in areas where it had its greatest impact. To provide the widest and most representative picture, the sources include letters, oral testimony, government records, and memoirs. Songs and poetry demonstrate people's feelings toward colonialism, while pictures from everyday life—including schools, dress, houses, sports, and ordinary objects—further show us society in the imperial age. They demonstrate that imperialism was more than the preoccupation of explorers and government officials. It saturated ordinary experience.

Imperialism was a disorganized phenomenon involving incredible violence, plunder, resistance, and heated debate. It involved state power and private enterprise but it also led to changes in culture and society. Primary documents can capture some of that chaos and uncertainty, and they can portray both the wealth and the pain imperialism brought with it. While some people at the time had firm beliefs about the European, Japanese, and U.S. expansion, others were confused about the economic, technological, and cultural developments that brought about rapidly changing ways of life. Some of these attitudes remain to challenge us, as we ponder the relationship between industrialized and agrarian countries. The environment, the use of machinery, and racial, national, religious, or regional identity remain vital issues to this day.

Categories of People

The two people in this picture are quite distinct by gender, race, and attire. A man garbed in Indian military clothing stands by, straight and sturdy, while a woman sits, hunched over in concentration. From what we know about the 19th-century role of each gender, there is something odd in the categories of people, for the man should be working, with the woman standing at his side or perhaps even absent from the photo. The inversion of gender might tell us that normal gender rules worked differently under empire. In last third of the 19th century the races are together in this depiction, also portraying a certain vision of what the empire was supposed to mean to people.

Orientation of Figures

Although these two figures inhabit the same photo, they are apart from one another and almost seem to live in different worlds. The orientation of the figures suggests a separateness that empire brought while unifying peoples. Simultaneously the attentive Indian guard allows Queen Victoria to work in confidence—an attitude that mirrors many Europeans' belief that only empire would protect the colonized people from harm.

Reason for Taking Photos

Photography recorded reality for all kinds of people to observe. It preserved scenes, events, and people for future generations, and it made people believe that they were witnessing an actual truth or reality. But official photos were also taken to convey messages, which could be different from the truth. This photo could convey information about the queen's attentiveness to her royal duties, but it could also convey a message about British imperial power.

Audience

This magazine was intended for well-educated Indian women who wanted to read, not just amuse themselves with pictures. It was also intended for those who *could* read and had some knowledge of the West, as indicated by the western clothes worn by the woman on the cover. Many documents without an apparent audience have one: letters in a person's handwriting suggest a familiarity with that handwriting and thus, often, an intimate reader. Printed or typewritten or other machine-generated texts suggest a wider, less familiar audience.

Design

In keeping with the taste of its audience, the design of this cover combines pleasant graphics with a female figure and a printed list of the articles contained within. This design suggests the wish to attract a middle-class readership, as well as an ambition to show that accessible knowledge is between the covers of the journal.

THE INDIAN LADIES' MAGAZINE

Vol. I.]   AUGUST, 1901.   [No. 2.

CONTENTS.

Introduction

Imperialism in the Modern Age

World history provides many examples of vast empires, including those of the ancient Romans, the Moguls of India, and the Ottomans, based in present-day Turkey. In the late 15th century European states—Portugal, Spain, France, the Netherlands, and England—started a new phase of imperial development when they began sending their people to many parts of the world in hopes of profiting from trade and obtaining valuables such as gold. The expansion of Europe to the New World in search of riches is a familiar story. Religious authorities undertook to Christianize the indigenous, or local, peoples, further adding to the colonizing impulse. By the 18th century, Russia was expanding its territorial borders southward into more of Asia. All these efforts can be seen as an old-fashioned form of colonization based on the somewhat limited vision of traders, missionaries, and government officials.

All that changed in the 19th century. Historians pinpoint the high tide of modern imperialism as falling between roughly 1870 and the 1930s, when the European powers finally took political control of most of the globe and Japan joined them by annexing Korea, Taiwan, and other Asian peoples. For much of the century, economic growth beyond Europe's borders escalated, colonial armies expanded, and growing national bureaucracies worked to tame what they called colonial chaos. At issue in the new imperialism was promoting modern state power, ensuring national prosperity, and making citizens feel that their nation was better because it had colonies. "Japanese imperialism is not based on momentary whims," a leading journalist announced. "It is a policy born out of necessity if we are to exist as a nation and survive as a race." The great powers came to believe that only having large empires would guarantee their status in the future.

The imperialists justified their expansion and conquest in a variety of ways. For centuries Western expansion had aimed to create wealth for a limited number of monarchs and traders, but modern industry changed all that. The industrial revolution that began in England in the 18th century and then spread across the European continent increased economic competition. New inventions made businessmen even hungrier for sources of raw materials, while booms and busts in the economic cycle made them desperate for a wider base of secure markets. The need for food spiraled with the surging European population and its increasing concentration in industrial cities—again an opportunity for traders. To gain control, the imperialists used their new technological advantages in steamships, weaponry, and railroads as powerful, invasive wedges through foreign lands and peoples. Establishing political power over larger territories and more ethnic groups would help them achieve this security of resources and trade, help them reach their goals of profit and industrial progress.

Competition among nations for political power also fueled the new imperialism. In the 18th and early 19th centuries, political revolutions to modernize the state and to install new concepts of citizenship whose watchword was the brotherhood of man took place. Later in the 19th century, Europeans became less inclined to view the state as a bulwark of individuals' rights. Instead their leaders accepted international power politics as part of building a modern state. Gaining colonies was one part of this new international competition among modernizing nation-states. Britain took over Egypt, large sections of the Near East, and much of the coast of East Africa to keep its interests in India safe from other European states. Japan annexed nearby areas in order to build a thick perimeter that would protect it from the rapacious Europeans.

If concepts of the brotherhood of man disappeared from intra-European politics, Western beliefs in natural rights did not apply to the colonized. Imperialists did not look at the seizure of land, buildings, or artworks as theft, but as justifiable confiscation by those who would presumably make the best use of the land or who were civilized enough to appreciate works of art. In contrast,

In 1911 Africa was divided among the Western powers into French Sudan, French Congo, Belgian Congo, German Southwest Africa, German East Africa, and British East Africa. Asia was similarly governed by foreigners. Chinese patriots lamented their country's being "carved up like a melon."

This 18th-century Chinese plate, used in the ordinary course of life, depicts European merchants inspecting goods in a chinaware shop. The presence of Westerners became part of everyday culture, even in those places thought to be immune from their influence.

they believed, the indigenous peoples needed the benefits of European culture, especially the Christian religion and the work ethic. The Germans and the Japanese felt that their "scientific" bureaucracies could regularize the rulership of inferior peoples. Nineteenth- and 20th-century rule came to revolve increasingly around racist tenets that were developed from the theories of Charles Darwin and scientists and social scientists influenced by his theories of the uneven evolution of species. Darwin saw human development, like that of other species of animals and plants, as taking place in a context of brutal natural conditions and competition. Influenced by Darwin's thought, the imperialists accepted that warfare among different groups for survival was inherent in the human species too. Although under early colonialism people certainly saw distinctions among peoples around the world, in the 19th century science developed racist concepts and vocabularies from which arose the modern notion that some races are biologically inferior to others. Racism flourished among both Western and Eastern imperialists.

The impetus for trade and conquest came from elite groups such as politicians and merchants, but imperialism was also a popular phenomenon, one that captured the imagination of Europeans and stoked their appetites for new goods. From the beginning of the expansion for trade, upper-class Europeans had enjoyed the availability of new products such as spices and exotic plants. Sugar, tobacco, tea, coffee, and an array of pain-killing drugs such as opium had become household necessities by the 19th century. But being members of nations that owned colonies also became a source of pride. Japanese citizens, like the English working classes, applauded their armies' victories in the race for colonies. Such victories stimulated national pride and could even dull resentment of urban crowding, unemployment, or the other difficulties of living in a rapidly changing industrial society. Many bureaucrats, soldiers, and traders who engaged in imperialism went out simply to know more about the world. In doing so they grew more confident that they themselves were superior to Africans and Asians and that their rule was beneficial for the subject peoples. Imperialism thus had a wide-ranging, paradoxical impact on identity, making imperialist peoples more nationalistic while providing them with a more varied diet, lifestyle, and knowledge—all of them derived from other complex cultures.

However much the imperializing populations paraded their superiority, in fact they acquired more than the raw materials of

underdeveloped societies. From the earliest European colonization of the New World, the goods bought and stolen there were a
source of inspiration and delight: "All the days of my life I have
seen nothing that rejoiced my heart so much," the artist Albrecht
Dürer had written in 1520 on seeing artworks from Mexico. "I
marveled at the subtle *Ingenia* [spirit or genius] of men in foreign
lands." From then on, Europeans became utterly dependent on
others, borrowing heavily from the highest forms of culture found
in Africa, Asia, and Latin America. Eighteenth-century pottery
manufacturers in England and on the continent learned to make
better porcelain and china using Chinese techniques, while textile
designs and procedures from a variety of Asian manufacturers
were copied by early entrepreneurs of the industrial revolution in
England and France. By the end of the 19th century, painters,
musicians, and philosophers were drawing on the colonies to
update their ideas and styles. What has come to be called modern
art in Europe developed from imitating the art of non-Europeans.
Museums, zoos, circuses, and colonial expositions displaying a
variety of global artifacts, art, and animals shaped leisure time
among Westerners. Europeans stole outright many possessions
from their colonies, or acquired them at rock-bottom prices if
they paid anything at all. The debts of Western and Japanese
imperialists to the rest of the world are long-standing and can
never be repaid.

It is right to emphasize the brute force that the imperialists
exercised on colonized peoples. Whether English, Japanese, or
Russian, they impoverished, mistreated, and oppressed indigenous
peoples. Imperial relationships were more complex than this,
however. For one thing, the imperialists dealt with highly developed societies in Africa, Asia, the Near East, and elsewhere; they
bargained with and used the knowledge of these societies' powerful leaders. They also met resistance to their attempted conquests
at every turn in the 19th and early 20th centuries: colonial warfare
never stopped, and peace never really came.

The colonized peoples could exercise a different kind of hold
over their colonizers, the case of modern art being but one example. They also appropriated and borrowed from their masters in
their architecture and art, setting the stage for the more hybrid, global culture of the late 20th century. Like the Arab trader Tippo Tip in
Africa, many added to their wealth by dealing with the imperial
powers, while others adopted Western dress and customs, seeing
this not only as advantageous to their careers but interpreting it as
superior to their own traditions. Serving the imperial powers as

This life-sized South Asian sculpture of a tiger killing an Englishman belonged to Tipu Sultan, ruler of Mysore, whom the British killed in 1799. Even before the days of high imperialism, feelings ran high and violence infused European expansion.

local administrators, such as tax collectors and judges, or as soldiers in colonial armies, the colonized peoples came to acquire Western education and to learn about Western economic and political systems. In fact, some historians see these indigenous bureaucrats as the lynchpins of imperialism without whom it could not have functioned. Although naturally they contested imperial rule and chafed under it, colonized peoples also constructed their own vision of what a return to independence would be, often enlisting ideas of the imperialists, such as nationalism, in their plans. By the end of the 19th century the middle and upper classes in Asia, Africa, and elsewhere had developed sophisticated political parties and other organizations to promote their liberation.

As the 20th century opened, imperialism had taken an array of individual twists and turns. Colonized people were resisting the imperial powers in greater numbers, and it was clear to many that the imperialists exercised less successful control than they thought. As hatred of imperial domination became more vocal and open resistance grew, the costs of empire increased, if only in terms of expanded armies, weaponry, and casualties. Growing competition among industrializing nations for empire increased the costs still more, as each felt a need for huge battleships to patrol the seas to safeguard their possessions. Not only were Europeans fighting each other for imperial gains, but in 1904 and 1905 the Japanese—a non-European imperial upstart—defeated the Russian empire in a bloody war for a controlling position in East Asia. The West understandably reeled at the import of this defeat, for national liberation movements quickened the pace of resistance thereafter.

Inspired by the Japanese victory over Russia, the Young Turks, a group of reform-minded army officers, tried to make a modern empire out of the extensive Ottoman holdings in the Middle East. The outbreak of World War I in Europe deepened imperial dependence on the colonies for both manpower and resources. But at the same time, the war weakened their grip on colonial power, because the war cost them so much in manpower and resources while the colonies themselves gained. As the European nations poured their resources into destroying one another, the non-Western nations enlarged their share of global trade. Colonized men, such as Africans from Senegal fighting for the French in Europe, came to crave full citizenship or independence as their reward. Paradoxically, World War I both fed the need for colonies and hastened their demise.

During the 1920s and 1930s, as the contradictions of imperialism became more apparent, the masses in the colonies began joining national liberation movements and demanding their own identities back. In India, Mohandas K. ("Mahatma," or "great souled") Gandhi made the most dramatic use of mass discontent with his innovative political tactic of nonviolent civil disobedience. Returning soldiers and middle-class intellectuals alike protested the new mandate system, which turned colonies that had been promised independence into protectorates or "mandates" set up by the victorious powers in the Peace of Paris. This system kept most old colonies under strict control and parceled out Germany's possessions as well. Reactions were violent, but usually futile. The victorious great powers—notably Britain and France—had been sorely tested in the war and were loath to relax their grip on empire. For one thing, they were in debt, and when the Great Depression broke out in the 1930s they felt an even stronger need to cement their colonies to them. Japan and Italy went to war for new conquests, expanding their reach still further even as the tide was turning sharply against empire. Later, in the aftermath of World War II, national liberation groups were mostly able to overthrow the imperial powers in a process called decolonization. Although the seeds of decolonization by national liberation groups had been planted from the beginnings of imperialism, the story of their full flowering after 1945 will not be part of our story.

The history of imperialism has many plots and subplots. One plot follows the violent appropriation of lands, the slaughter of local peoples, and attempts to eradicate many of their ways. Another plot could show indigenous peoples benefiting from improved sanitation, hospitals, urban development, railroads, and expanded trade. Still another might travel through a landscape of urban slums showing unemployed and uprooted rural peoples who had lost their land to developers, bureaucrats, or white settlers. Or it might progress through the museums or households of Europe, where it would be hard not to find brilliant signs of the globalization of culture brought about by imperialism. Those who have fought for freedom from the economic and political impact of imperialism have told the story in still other ways, and those who have felt most tellingly its cultural and social effects recount many different tales. The documents that follow will provide many accounts from around the globe of this exceedingly complex phenomenon, though the dominant voices are those of people who had some degree of power and controlled the pens.

Of late, 'tis true, quite sick of Rome and Greece
We fetch our models from the wise Chinese;
European artists are too cool and chaste
For Mand'rin is the only man of taste.

—James Cawthorn,
"Of Taste" (1756)

Chapter One

On the Brink of Modern Empire

I n the 18th century, more and more Europeans came to drink two very foreign beverages—coffee and tea—both made with boiling-hot water. The custom of taking these two drinks transformed patterns of behavior, as people in the West opened coffeehouses and cafes where they sat debating politics in new ways while they sipped their bitter brews. Teatime became an important social ritual providing an occasion for neighborliness and family intimacy. An age of political debate leading to democratic revolutions thus opened, as did an era of more closely knit family life. The use of boiling water that killed bacteria is also believed to have caused mortality to plummet in the 18th century, and population to surge. The brisk trade in tea and coffee, grown outside Europe but fast becoming a necessity for Westerners, changed history.

The actual tea and coffee as well as the knowledge of their uses came from European contacts with Asia, the Middle East, and North Africa. From the 16th through the 18th century, Europeans developed a variety of colonial systems and had a wide array of interactions with non-Europeans, not just military and economic but cultural as well. These contacts were global. Spanish and Portuguese monarchs had brutally conquered and ruled most of South and Central America since the early 16th century, but by the 18th century these powers' prosperity was rapidly declining. Rising nations such as the English, French, and Dutch had developed strong trading relations in Asia, Africa, the Caribbean, and North America. They established colonies to guarantee ongoing trade and the continued production of raw materials like sugar.

By the beginning of the 19th century the West had acquired broad knowledge from non-Europeans, and the way of life in Europe had

Seventeenth-century Europeans learned about the latest customs sprouting from overseas trade from illustrated books. This drawing taught them how to serve the popular new products coffee, tea, and chocolate and depicted their origins in Arab, Chinese, and Aztec cultures.

Asian, African, and Middle Eastern cultures influenced motifs for china, such as the head of a bird for a spout on this teapot. Such sophisticated pottery developed in 18th-century Europe after businessmen learned techniques of East Asian production.

Invention of the Teabag

Experimentation and dumb luck led to the invention of teabags. In 1908, customers of an American tea merchant received small samples of tea wrapped in silk pouches and not sent, as was customary, in the more expensive tins. The customers were baffled but decided to try dunking the packets in a teapot of boiling water. From the merchant's attempt to save on the cost of tin containers, the teabag was born.

been transformed by the availability of outside foodstuffs like sugar, chocolate, potatoes, tomatoes, and corn. Trade with China brought knowledge of its sophisticated production of dishware. Asian cotton became a model for Western design and helped inspire the industrial revolution in textiles. Medical, scientific, and cultural knowledge also influenced European customs, interior design, and the fine arts.

The influential political thinkers of the 18th century in Europe were part of the Enlightenment, a movement that opposed traditional (what it called magical) religious practices and the grip that clergymen had on people's minds. Thus, Asian religions and philosophies like Confucianism appealed to them. Thinkers of the Enlightenment wanted to make monarchies more "constitutional" (that is, governed by a fundamental set of laws) and rational, and to reform the economy. The founders of new economic policies developed the idea of "free trade" or laissez-faire (from the French, "let people do as they choose") from the Chinese system in which the government let the economy move freely instead of regulating it. This concept was in contrast to the trade monopolies and guild systems that European governments enforced. Gradually, the Chinese civil service system in which people gained government jobs based on the result of examinations replaced the European system of bribery and family influence peddling. Some historians claim that before the 19th century Europeans gave non-Western cultures more respect than they ever would after. But the borrowing of non-Western ideas as the basis for Western civilization never stopped. Indeed, Europeans needed and relied on the rest of the world.

Culture flowed both ways: from the 16th through the 18th century the Chinese, for instance, took an intense interest in Western science and religion. More importantly for their own economic future, many Japanese were developing a deep interest in Western technology and arts. Trade in European weapons was brisk, while Africans and Asians often snapped up European iron goods and cheap textiles.

For Europeans, international exposure had as one crucial base the economic advantages it would bring. In the 18th century the vicious but profitable slave trade boomed with the expansion of colonies in the Caribbean and North America and the development of cotton manufacturing. Many nations participated in the trade, but by this time the British were the leading merchants of African slaves for the New World. European and Ottoman slavers bought tens of thousands of Africans, mostly from other African merchants who participated in a highly developed trade feeding the global market in slaves. The economic advantages brought by global commerce led to great wars, most notably in the 17th and 18th centuries among the French, the British, and sometimes the Dutch. During these centuries Britain's East India Company allied itself with Indian merchants and ambitious princes who had their own armies to secure trade throughout much of South Asia from all other rivals.

The prelude to full-scale imperialism consisted of this vast range of cultural interactions, struggles for power and profit, and bloody warfare in all parts of the globe. The "new imperialism" of the late 19th century involved a massive drive to conquer and rule Africa and Asia, but for the moment European trade and colonization did not yet mean building vast, distant political empires on those continents. Instead, the rising powers were developing a cultural and economic dependence on the rest of the world.

Vital Knowledge

Medical and other practical knowledge was part of the cultural and economic dependence that developed in Europe. Lady Mary Wortley Montagu, an English aristocrat, relished her life as a diplomat's wife in Turkey early in the 18th century. Studying Arabic and Turkish culture, she was one of the few Westerners to enter the harem—the secluded living quarters of the rulers' wives—and provided important and positive descriptions of that institution. She wrote many letters to her friends in high court society and introduced a great deal of new knowledge into England, most importantly the procedures for smallpox inoculation. This advance helped lessen the scourge of what was then a disfiguring if not always killing disease.

Adrianople, April 1 [1717]

I am going to tell you a thing that I am sure will make you wish yourself here. The small-pox, so fatal, and so general amongst us, is here entirely harmless by the invention of *ingrafting*, which is the term they give it. There is a set of old women who make it their business to perform the operation every autumn, in the month of September, when the great heat is abated. People send to one another to know if any of their family has a mind to have the small-pox: they make parties for this purpose, and when they are met (commonly fifteen or sixteen together), the old woman

"In an uncultivated, vulgar person the desire for material gain is always stronger than fear of the law; this is especially true of merchants, who often view law as a mere formality which can be violated at will."

—Li Shih-Yao, on the need to control British and other European traders in China, 1759

From the tulips of the Middle East to geraniums like this one found in Africa, imperialist Europe became dense with flowers, whether in newly created flower gardens or on wallpaper, dress fabric, or linens. Before colonial expansion Europeans had contented themselves with gardens of vegetables and medicinal herbs.

comes with a nut-shell full of the matter of the best sort of small-pox, and asks what veins you please to have opened. She immediately rips open what you offer to her with a large needle (which gives you no more pain than a common scratch), and puts into the vein as much venom as can lie upon the head of her needle, and after binds up the little wound with a hollow bit of shell; and in this manner opens four or five veins. The Grecians have commonly the superstition of opening one in the middle of the forehead, in each arm, and on the breast, to mark the sign of the cross; but this has a very ill effect, all these wounds leaving little scars, and is not done by those that are not superstitious who choose to have them in the legs, or that part of the arm that is concealed. The children or young patients play together all the rest of the day, and are in perfect health to the eighth. Then the fever begins to seize them, and they keep their beds two days, very seldom three. They have very rarely above twenty or thirty in their faces, which never mark; and in eight days' time they are as well as before their illness. . . . You may believe I am very well satisfied of the safety of the experiment, since I intend to try it on my dear little son.

I am patriot enough to take pains to bring this useful invention into fashion in England; and I should not fail to write to some of our doctors very particularly about it, if I knew any one of them that I thought had virtue enough to destroy such a considerable branch of their revenue for the good of mankind.

Since the first explorations by Europeans in the late 15th and early 16th centuries, expansion had brought much-needed food crops like corn, potatoes, and tomatoes to Europe. As a result, food became more abundant and diets more varied, and nutrition improved. In the 18th century the African Association of Britain sent the explorer Mungo Park to chart the Niger River for such purposes. In the same century, kings and princes sent out plant hunters such as André Michaux of France to deserts, mountains, and the tropics to collect plants, seeds, and cuttings for the gardens of their royal patrons. Such lavish botanical gardens as those at Kew outside London and others in Paris were developed to expand general horticultural and botanical knowledge as part of the Enlightenment thirst to advance science, improve life, and make money.

Besides providing food, the flood of new plants also changed middle- and upper-class Europeans' lifestyles. Before this time, aristocrats had generally surrounded their large

estates with "parks," or broad expanses of grass and lawns. What gardens they did have were often stiffly geometric arrangements of hedges and walks. The range of plants native to Europe was small, and gardens bloomed for only short periods of time in late spring. Plants found worldwide brought the modern garden into being, because they offered a blossoming season that went from early spring through fall. The resulting lush gardens and new public parks abandoned the formal style for one modeled on the more naturalistic, irregular lines used by the Chinese. Thus there developed the "English" garden of wandering paths, grottoes, and meandering brooks.

The plans for all these gardens and parks resulted from the reports of plant hunters and naturalists. Besides his trip to Persia and Madagascar, the French botanist Michaux visited North America, and he introduced many plants from around the world to horticultural enthusiasts. His letters reporting on his scientific travel, along with the specimens he sent back home, whetted Europe's appetite and were thus an important part of the prelude to imperialism. The first below was written to the botanist André Thouin on July 30, 1782.

I cannot express to you the delight with which I run about the country here. In examining the multitude of plants with which the fields abound, I was often transported beyond myself, and compelled to pause and tranquilize my mind for some moments. At night I could not sleep but awaited the dawn of day with impatience. What happiness! to find myself in Asia, and at my pleasure to traverse the mountains and valleys covered with liliaceaous plants, orchideae, daphnes, laurus, vitices, myrtles, andrachnes, styrax, palms, and other vegetable productions, different from those of Europe.

This letter, written January 14, 1783, was addressed to the brother of King Louis XVI.

The seeds that I have the honor to send to you, Monsieur, have been collected during the crossing of the desert from Aleppo to Baghdad. I would have liked to add a large herbarium but most of the plants were withered and the shrubby trees denuded of leaves. There are several very interesting ones whose seeds I have been able to gather only by searching for a considerable time at the foot of the plant and in places where I surmised the wind would have

"I am afraid the cutting of the great Toxicodendron [poison ivy] is perished; for it lay at the bottom of the box, where there had been wet. I am very desirous to get all the species of this genus."
—Letter from botanist Philip Miller to a plant hunter, January 12, 1758

brought them together. I beg you to believe that I have made every possible effort; I was often obliged to turn aside from the caravan which always followed its route, and to avoid being surprised by Arabs or ferocious beasts, especially beside the Euphrates, I took the precaution of being well armed.

I have gathered more than a hundred kinds of seeds, and I have put together in the same package the most interesting ones. I have put separately those of which I have been able to procure samples to make a herbarium. I presume all these plants can survive in the Orangery and a few will succeed out of doors. . . .

Mixed Responses to Europeans

Although cultural interaction has gone on for thousands of years, the expansion of trade, travel, and cultural ties that had intensified from the 16th century on brought mutual scrutiny and judgment of how others lived. Cultural interactions broadened knowledge around the globe and brought opportunities for new self-definition. People could think of changing the way they lived and thought, or they could become protective of their customs. Whatever side they took, more people were aware that there were cultural alternatives to their own political, religious, and social beliefs.

Travelers to Europe from the Islamic world of the Middle East and Africa often saw Europeans as defiled by Christianity; in places where Islamic culture had once thrived they were upset to see the desecration of former places of worship. Al-Ghazā, a visitor to Spain from Morocco in the mid 18th century, was shocked at what he saw there. Often the long-standing view of European culture as being barbaric blocked any accurate assessment of the military power that the Western powers had been amassing.

Their dwellings have windows overlooking the street, where the women sit all the time, greeting the passersby. Their husbands treat them with the greatest courtesy. The women are very much addicted to conversation and conviviality with men other than their husbands, in company or in private. They are not restrained from going wherever they think fit. It often happens that a Christian returns to his home and finds his wife or his daughter or his sister in the company of another Christian, a stranger, drinking together and leaning against one another. He is delighted with

A Muslim woman is covered from head to toe, according to Islamic dress requirements for appearances in public. As they learned the languages and literatures of the people they encountered in trade, Europeans became fascinated with their culture, customs, and—to imperialist eyes—unusual clothing.

this and, according to what I am told, he esteems it as a favor from the Christian who is in the company of his wife. . . .

When the party dispersed we returned to our lodgings and we prayed to God to save us from the wretched state of these infidels who are devoid of manly jealousy and are sunk in unbelief and we implored the Almighty not to hold us accountable for our offense in conversing with them as the circumstances required.

For others, European ways offered points for reform and change in their own culture. In the 18th century, Japanese intellectuals commented favorably on European alphabets and artistic techniques, even though the common view today is that Japan was "closed" to outside influence. The Japanese printmaker Hokusai introduced the European sense of depth into his famous prints, while Japanese intellectuals and scholars, such as Morishima Churyo in the document below, found the Latin-derived European alphabet far superior to the Chinese characters from which the Japanese written language was adapted. Such openness to new ideas, historians believe, prepared Japan for its rapid modernization and its own quest for empire a century later.

In a Dutch book that describes the customs of all countries, the use of Chinese characters is ridiculed in these terms: In China a character is used for every object and thing. Some characters have only one meaning, whereas others are used to express ten or 20 ideas. There are probably tens of thousands of them. Even though the natives of China study them day and night, so earnestly that they forget about sleeping and eating, they are unable to learn in the course of a lifetime all the elements in their country's writing. This means that few people can easily read books written in their own tongue. This is the height of the ridiculous. In Europe, twenty-five letters are not considered inadequate.

I believe that in the olden days writing was simple, and no characters were ever used. In later times, Chinese characters were borrowed to indicate the fifty sounds of Japanese. In subsequent generations Chinese characters came to be used for meaning as

Familiarity between the sexes in the West shocked visitors from Asian cultures. European men and women participated in dancing, games of cards, village festivals and fairs, and socializing at home that often seemed uncivilized and even immoral to non-European travelers.

well as sound, and the national custom of using only a few easy characters was abandoned in favor of the complicated and troublesome Chinese system. Why was this?

The White Peril

The Chinese had a long history of trade and exploration, but they had also controlled access to their country by foreign traders from the Ottoman and Indian empires. They did the same with the British in the 18th century, limiting their trade to the port of Canton. As they expanded their trading capacity, the British chafed under these restrictions, while the Chinese viewed with alarm the persistent attempts to infiltrate other ports. Here one 18th-century Chinese bureaucrat organizes a new set of regulations ("Five Rules to Regulate Foreigners," 1759) for controlling these incursions. Some historians have viewed such regulations as signs that the Chinese were hopelessly backward and narrow-minded. Others, however, suggest that their concerns were natural ones for keeping social life orderly and maintaining political control. Long before the European population exploded in the 18th century, the Chinese population had grown rapidly too. Instead of meeting change with change, the government tried to keep order through a variety of means such as limiting potential troublemakers' access to society.

Chinese regulations restricted foreign traders to designated buildings on Shameen Island facing Guangzhou, so that the government could monitor commerce and prevent disorderly conduct. But the European powers aimed to expand trade, even if it meant war.

Foreigners who live in the distant seas do not normally understand the Chinese language. Formerly, when they came to Canton to trade, they relied upon Chinese translators to conduct their business. Lately foreign merchants like Hung Jen-hui [James Flint] have proved to be not only familiar with Cantonese as well as Mandarin but also able to read Chinese words and understand their meanings. There are several who have achieved this proficiency. How could they possibly have achieved it, had not some traitorous Chinese secretly taught them? . . .

Since foreigners are outside the sphere of civilization, there is no need for them to have any contact with our people other than business transactions, whenever they come to China for trade purposes. . . . The following rules, in the judgment of your humble servant, are both simple and practical enough to be adopted. They are presented here for Your Majesty's consideration.

1. Foreigners should never be allowed to stay at Canton during the winter.

Normally foreign ships arrive at Canton in the fifth or sixth month and sail for home in the ninth or tenth month. Even if foreigners have to stay through the winter on account of business, they move from Canton to Macao after their ships have sailed for home. Lately many foreign traders, under the pretext that some of their merchandise has not been sold or that their debtors have failed to discharge their obligations in full, entrust their ships and cargoes to the care of other merchants who proceed home, while they themselves stay on in Canton. During their stay they devote themselves to the study of the prices of various goods in different provinces. . . .

Canton, being the capital of a province, is too important a place to allow foreigners to stay there on a permanent basis, since permanent residence will enable them to spy on our activities. From now on, when a foreign trader arrives at Canton, the Co-hong merchants should sell all of his goods as quickly as possible, pay him immediately, . . . so that he can return home. . . .

2. While in Canton, foreigners should be ordered to reside in Co-hong headquarters so that their conduct can be carefully observed and strictly regulated. . . .These foreigners often become drunk and commit breaches of the peace; sometimes they also visit houses of prostitution. Their behaviour in this regard is of course extremely improper.

. . . .Among the foreigners the British are the most violent and are prone to recreate incidents.

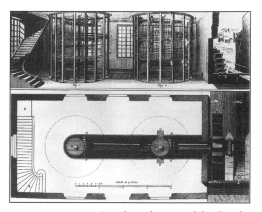

An industrial spy revealed to British producers the secret of this Italian machine for making silk, an idea that had in turn come from China. Imperialist interest in Asian techniques for making silk ran high because of the profits to be made from the luxury trades.

This so-called man-ape, drawn in 1749, was actually a chimpanzee. In the West, scholarly interest in plant and animal species had increased during the Scientific Revolution of the 1700s.

Figuring Out Differences

Europe in the 18th century saw people rethinking the nature of government, religion, and social structure. Moved by expanding trade and colonization, they continued to puzzle over global social, cultural, climatic, geographic, and racial differences. The Dutch, who in this period were prime Western slave traders and active colonizers, took a particular interest in why blacks and whites were unlike. In this encyclopedia account, white superiority differs from more modern racism in that scientists attempt to find biological justification for calling other races inferior.

Negroes have possibly been on the earth just as long as Whites. The almost six thousand years which have passed between the first man and us prevent us from knowing if he was white or black. The holy scriptures are completely silent in this regard. However, we may with good reason think that he was white; firstly because Negroes are seldom seen beyond the lands between the tropics. Adam was formed and lived four hundred miles to the North of the Tropic of Cancer. Secondly, seldom, if ever, has the Negroes' color been known to pale through a change in climate, while Whites become yellower as they near the scorching climate. This one observation is sufficient in order to conclude with certainty that blacks must be descendant from whites and must have acquired the darker color which distinguishes them over the course of the centuries. Thirdly, there are far fewer Negroes than whites. Almost all the territories inhabited by Negroes are known; their area is about two million square miles, while the territories occupied by whites comprise more than eight million square miles.

One very influential European way of looking at cultural differences involved seeing some societies in Africa and Asia as freer than European ones. In the state of nature, reform-minded thinkers maintained, one had natural rights—rights that had been lost in the rise of powerful European states. "Man is born free and everywhere he is in chains," as one French reformer put it. During the Enlightenment that followed from the coming of modern science, liberty from tyrannical rule became an important rallying cry for political and economic reformers. This concept motivated the

American and French Revolutions, along with a host of other uprisings inspired by their success.

But the so-called "noble savages" whose "natural rights" revolutionaries admired and even enshrined in the U.S. Constitution disappeared, replaced by the actual Africans enslaved on New World plantations. When the French made their famous "Declaration of the Rights of Man" in 1789 during the French Revolution, various groups immediately debated whether Jews, women, blacks, and slaves could have the same rights. Among the many issues raised in these debates was that of the fate of the prosperous sugar colonies like St. Domingue (the island now shared by Haiti and the Dominican Republic) and Martinique in the Caribbean, and of slavery in them. Here a French lawyer and politician, Antoine Pierre Barnave, argues in 1790 to keep both colonies and slaves and to prevent the "Rights of Man" from applying to them.

The interest of the French nation in supporting its commerce, preserving its colonies, and favoring their prosperity by every means compatible with the interests of the metropole [the French nation] has appeared to us, from every angle of vision, to be an incontestable truth. . . .

Abandon the colonies, and these sources of prosperity will disappear or diminish.

Abandon the colonies, and you will import, at great price, from foreigners what they buy today from you. . . .

Here then, Sirs, is the project for a decree that your committee has unanimously voted to propose to you:

The National Assembly, deliberating on the addresses and petitions from the cities of commerce and manufacturing . . . and on the representations made by the deputies from the colonies.

Declares that, considering the colonies as a part of the French empire, and desiring to enable them to enjoy the fruits of the happy regeneration that has been accomplished in the empire, it never intended to include them in the constitution that it has decreed for the kingdom or to subject them to laws which might be incompatible with their particular, local proprieties. . . .

"All mortals are equal. It is not birth but virtue that makes for difference among them," reads the caption of this engraving. A woman representing love of country measures a black man and a white equally, in line with Enlightenment beliefs in liberty and equality.

Moreover, the National Assembly declares that it never intended to introduce innovations into any of the branches of indirect or direct commerce between France and its colonies [thus it leaves the slave trade untouched] and hereby puts the colonists and their properties under the special protection of the nation and declares criminal, toward the nation, whoever works to excite uprisings against them.

Freedom's Ferment

In the midst of these revolutionary debates, slaves in the French colony of Saint Domingue rebelled against their masters. Unable to suppress the uprising, the French government formally abolished slavery in 1794, an act that inspired one of the generals leading the Saint Domingue uprising, François Joseph Toussaint L'Ouverture, to shift his allegiance back to France. Toussaint L'Ouverture became governor of the colony, but resistance to the planters and the French continued, because the conditions of freedom remained oppressive.

In 1802 Napoleon, soon to become emperor of France, sent troops to reestablish full control of the colony for the planters and himself. Though Toussaint was captured, a group of insurgent generals fought on, defeating Napoleon's armies and establishing the Republic of Haiti in 1804. One of these generals, the former slave Henri Christophe, explained in a letter to a French counterpart how his commitment to the very principles of the French Revolution—citizenship, freedom, equality, family, and community—prevented him from surrendering. His and other writings associated with Haiti's revolution circulated to inspire slaves and other colonial subjects to rebel. This letter is from 1802.

Should I ever have refused to submit to the orders of the French general sent to this island by the First Consul of the Republic [Napoleon], if everything had not conspired to convince me that the meditated consolidation of the good order which reigned in this colony was nothing less than the destruction of our liberty, and the rights resulting from equality? It is true, as you say, I have declared my greatest desire was to see the French arrive, and to deposit in their hands the share of authority with which I was invested, and enjoy as a simple citizen the benefits of liberty and equality in the bosom of my family, in the midst of my fellow-citizens, provided that they too partook, with myself, of these sacred rights. A Frenchman, loving and respecting France, I joyfully entertained this hope, a hope that my confidence in the government of the mother country fostered and confirmed from day to day. I have never changed my inclination in that respect; but by what fatality is it that this hope has been deceived. . . . ? St. Domingo, wholly French, enjoyed, as you know, the profoundest tranquillity; there were no rebels to be found: by what fatal blindness, then, did it happen, that France has come with all the terrors of war and the artillery of destruction? Not to subdue the rebels, (for rebels there were none) but to create amongst a peaceable people, and furnish a pretext to destroy or enslave them.

. . . As for me, my ambition always consisted in meriting the honourable consideration of good men, in seeing my fellow citizens happy; in enjoying, in common with them, the sole title of free man, the sole rights of equality, in the bosom of my tranquil family, and in the circle of a few estimable men.

The "New World" Remakes Colonialism

Holding foreign colonies was a complicated business, as all the early colonial powers discovered. The United States broke away from Britain in 1776, and in the first three decades of the 19th century Latin Americans fought successfully to free themselves from the Spanish and Portuguese, who had colonized much of the region in the 16th century. From being the great power of the 16th century, Spain entered a period of decline. Nonetheless, it fought viciously, if unsuccessfully, to maintain its colonies.

As in the United States, the rebel leaders in the uprisings against the Spanish were generally descendants of the original settlers and conquerors. These Creoles, as the offspring of European settlers were called, had the same inspiration as the rebels in the United States: they craved political freedom for themselves and access to the economic opportunity brought by trade with the British, whose commerce was booming. They also sought a freer hand with the Indian and African workers who toiled on their large plantations.

The victory of these rebellions led to the creation of many independent countries—Paraguay, Uruguay, Bolivia, and others—that were usually run as dictatorships and oligarchies, or government by an elite few. Simultaneously,

El Libertador

Simón Bolívar was inspired by European political thought to lead a series of successful revolutions in South America against Spain between 1810 and 1824. A committed military leader, Bolívar had definite ideas about the future of Latin America, which turned him toward promoting unity among the newly independent states. As he became more dictatorial in his ways, however, rivals unseated him from the presidency of Greater Colombia (present-day Colombia, Venezuela, Ecuador, and Panama) and the union of these states disintegrated.

many of their leaders tied the newly independent countries to Britain, as merchants in India and elsewhere were doing. In 1813 the following newspaper article defended the struggle of Simón Bolívar against the Spanish, because it would create ties to the British. This process of bringing in a dominant power for the trading profit it would introduce is sometimes called neocolonialism or neoimperialism, because it throws off a relationship of colonial rule, only to substitute an exploitative economic relationship. The situation in Latin America also shows that the reasons for imperialism included not only a push from would-be colonizers in the imperial power—Britain, in this case—but from a global pull mechanism far away.

Let us rejoice . . . in the irresistible ascendancy that England is about to assume over both hemispheres in guarantee of universal freedom.

Our industry, hitherto of no value, and our lagging agriculture will shake off their apathy in response to the rewards afforded the farmer by the rise in the prices of the products he cultivates. Once the ports of continental Europe are thrown open to British vessels, our farmers will export our coffee, cacao, indigo, cotton, and the like, which are in great demand. Maritime commerce having been so long suppressed wherever the Napoleonic influence has extended, Europe has suffered the want of products which have become as primary a necessity for them as their exports are for us. This trade is the foundation for the prosperity of our commerce and agriculture.

The policies and the mercantile interests of England and Spain are diametrically opposed with respect to America. Spain, unable to keep us tranquilly enslaved, is now bent upon our destruction; England, favoring our independence, is interested in our prosperity. The northern and southern regions of the New World are determined to maintain their freedom at all costs.

The Monroe Doctrine

The success of the Latin American liberation armies, after years of struggle and repression, prompted a formal policy declaration from U.S. President James Monroe in 1823. The Monroe Doctrine was a response to almost two centuries of war among the European powers to colonize and control

different regions of the Western Hemisphere. Enforced by the British, who wanted to develop a flourishing trade with the newly liberated countries, the Monroe Doctrine was part of a diplomatic arrangement that kept the Western Hemisphere from being swept into the new imperialism of the next decades. Instead, a more modern kind of neocolonial commerce took shape in which Britain dumped its inexpensive manufactured goods such as textiles and small iron products in the new markets, pleasing the local merchants but driving many domestic Latin American manufacturers out of existence. The Monroe Doctrine had far-reaching economic consequences, because it made Latin Americans subservient to the economic might of Britain and other major powers.

"The American continents, by the free and independent condition which they have assumed and maintain, are henceforth not to be considered as subjects for future colonization by any European powers."

—The Monroe Doctrine, 1823

In the wars of the European powers in matters relating to themselves we have never taken any part nor does it comport with our policy to do so. It is only when our rights are invaded or seriously menaced that we resent injuries or make preparation for our defense. With the movements in this hemisphere we are of necessity more immediately connected, and by causes which must be obvious to all enlightened and impartial observers. The political system of the allied powers is essentially different in this respect from that of America. This difference proceeds from that which exists in their respective Governments; and to the defense of our own, which has been achieved by the loss of so much blood and treasure. . . . We owe it, therefore to candor and to the amicable relations existing between the United States and those powers to declare that we should consider any attempt on their part to extend their system to any portion of this hemisphere as dangerous to our peace and safety. With the existing colonies or dependencies of any European power we have not interfered and shall not interfere. But with the Governments who have declared their independence and maintained it, and whose independence we have, on great consideration and on just principles, acknowledged, we could not view any interposition for the purpose of oppressing them, or controlling in any other manner their destiny, by any European power in any other light than as the manifestation of an unfriendly disposition toward the United States.

A 19th-century Brazilian government official leads his household of family and slaves in a procession. Because of more interracial marriage in the former Portuguese and Spanish colonies, slaves were not always black and masters always white like their counterparts in the United States.

Chapter Two

Imperialism Takes Off

Awhole host of reasons is commonly given to explain the struggle for full-scale empire that became so heated in the 19th century: national pride, economic competition, the mission to Christianize the world, and continuing cultural curiosity. In general, however, the drive for money and might has received the most attention as the source of the drive for conquest. It motivated small powers like the Netherlands, Belgium, and Portugal as much as more prosperous and larger ones like Britain, France, and Russia to extend their political control internationally. Fledgling powers like Japan and the United States joined in later in the century.

Imperialism often involved domination of southern regions by more northerly powers. Britain was still working to achieve control of India when it took over Egypt, large parts of sub-Saharan Africa, and regions of Asia adjacent to India. Napoleon had excited the French over conquest in North Africa when he invaded Egypt late in the 18th century. In 1830 France started its campaign to conquer Algeria and by mid-century it was also engaged in West Africa and the Far East. Russia was continuing to move east against China and southward, absorbing the Muslim centers of Tashkent, Bukhara, Khiva, Geok-Tepe, and Merv between 1865 and 1884. As the century closed, the United States annexed Hawaii and moved against Spain, first eyeing the remnants of its empire, then defeating it in a war over Cuba and taking the Philippines.

Until recently, imperialism has been seen as a one-way operation in which industrial and military powers subdued savages who lacked economic and political leadership. Linked to that interpretation is the suggestion that imperialists then brought in effective government that allowed them to rule the native peoples fairly easily. Because these people lacked both culture and political institutions, the argument

By erecting monuments such as this one of Queen Empress Victoria in Calcutta the British government filled Indian cities with reminders of its sovereignty. They aimed to inspire awe and loyalty.

went, the imperial powers peacefully filled up an "empty" or "savage" territory, to that territory's benefit.

The truth is quite different. Along with bloodshed, imperialism generally brought chaos, as a result of overlapping systems of control. These systems included the demands of imperial masters and of local and regional rulers such as the chiefs of ethnic groups, nomadic warlords, slavers, and traders—all of whom claimed the right to direct, tax, or make indigenous peoples work for them.

Nor did the European powers or Japan have their own houses in order enough to claim the right to fill a supposed political vacuum. They were plagued by revolution, wars against one another, filth and disease, and constant social upheaval. In fact, for a country like France imperialism provided compensation for its defeat at the hands of Germany in 1871, while Japan saw imperialism late in the 19th century as a way of keeping occupied disgruntled and rebellious warriors who were causing trouble for those wanting the country to modernize through industrialization.

Despite its major impact, the big imperial scramble was not wholeheartedly approved—nor was it even a uniform policy. The military, explorers, entrepreneurs with their own armies, and missionaries often made conquests that their home governments approved only later. Missionaries were particularly effective at pulling in the powers to where they otherwise might not have gone, and even raised money to pay for colonial armies. The debates over imperialism were vociferous. The British muddled their way into an empire, debating all the way, which is not to say they took their colonies bloodlessly. Imperialism's territorial advance also depended on taking advantage of two notoriously weak empires, the Mogul in China and the Ottoman that extended through Asia Minor, the Middle East, and North Africa. Most of the documents shown here portray empires resolutely advancing from deliberately dispersed centers of imperial power, but this is not the entire picture. As in the case of China below, protest and resistance increasingly shaped the story too.

British Aggression in Asia and the Middle East

British, French, and U.S. traders, like the Spanish and Portuguese traders before them, made fortunes by trading opium to the Chinese, but in the first half of the 19th century the Chinese government became adamant that this rapidly growing trade stop. In previous centuries the trade had

brought the Chinese income, but now silver flowed out from the country as opium addiction gripped the country's population. But this addiction was not confined to the Chinese alone, for Westerners of all classes used opium, morphine, laudanum, and other opium-based products to dull the pain of headaches or toothaches, to quiet fussy children, or to serve as a source of inspiration to write books and poetry. The Chinese bureaucracy, however, sought to squash the trade by confiscating the opium and prohibiting further trade in it. No less than the future of China, they believed, was at stake.

As the major trader in opium by this time, the British government was committed to expanding free trade in opium products and especially to maintaining the flow of the vast amounts of silver from British commerce in opium produced in its Indian holdings. Instead of withdrawing from the Chinese market, Britain demanded concessions from the Chinese and the opening of even more new ports to the opium trade. The Chinese responded by twice declaring wars, conflicts that the British won after destroying Chinese property and fortifications. As a result of the first Opium War, in 1839–42, the British enforced the Treaty of Nanking, which gave it Hong Kong, guaranteed the opium trade, and opened four more ports to trade. The expanding commitment of the British government to the prosperity of its traders and the increased opportunity in China were crucial factors in the 19th-century growth of new empires built from the decline of others.

The Chinese had their own side of the story: in "The Evil of Opium" a typical Chinese bureaucrat analyzes the problem as one of inflation in the cost of silver and thus general inflation and declining prosperity.

Your Majesty's selfless and tireless devotion to the affairs of the state is motivated by your sincere desire to safeguard the welfare not only of all the people in China today but also of generations to come. Despite such diligence and earnestness on your part, the treasury does not have enough funds to meet expenses, and the livelihood of our people remains poor and unsatisfactory. Recently this situation has gone from bad to worse, and each year is worse than the year before. . . . As late as the Chia-ch'ing period [1796–1820] the nation was still economically sound, so sound that members of the gentry and wealthy merchants continued to live a life of luxury. What a different situation there is today. . . . Your humble servant has had occasion to notice that lately there

林文忠公
燒燬鴉片

道光十九年林文
忠公督兩廣此至
即查洋商所藏之鴉
片，查得二萬二百八
十三箱盡燒之于海口。
後有泊舟外洋，暗中輸
入者。公乘月黑潮退時，
出奇兵以搜之。役鴉其
船二十三艘于長沙灣之
邊，以此懷成交沙。鴉片
之進口日多，今則英國
政府已樂贊成。今思昔，
煙毒由今願除鴉片
人將成為欣者。

The Chinese government burned opium by the shipload in the 1800s. Concerned about the amount of money draining out of the country to support this expensive habit of some citizens, the government began seizing and destroying the product.

has been a steady increase in the price of silver in terms of standard coins, so great that one tael of silver is now worth more than 1,600 standard coins. The rise of the price of silver has nothing to do with the consumption of silver inside China; it results primarily from the outflow of silver to foreign countries. . . .

At the beginning, opium smoking was confined to the fops of wealthy families who took up the habit as a form of conspicuous consumption; even they knew that they should not indulge in it to the greatest extreme. Later, people of all social strata—from government officials and members of the gentry to craftsmen, merchants, entertainers, and servants, and even women, Buddhist monks and nuns, and Taoist priests—took up the habit and openly bought and equipped themselves with smoking instruments. Even in the center of our dynasty—the nation's capital and its surrounding areas—some of the inhabitants have also been contaminated by this dreadful poison.

The inflow of opium from foreign countries has steadily increased in recent years. . . . Conspiring with sea patrol and coast guards [whom they bribe], unscrupulous merchants at Canton use such small boats as "sneaking dragons" and "fast crabs" to ship silver out and bring opium in. From the third to the eleventh year of Tao-kuang [1823–31] the annual outflow of silver amounted to more than 17 million taels. From the eleventh to the fourteenth year [1831–34] it reached more than 20 million taels, and since the fourteenth year [1834] it has been more than 30 million taels. Large as they are, these figures do not cover the import of opium in other ports such as those in Fukien, Chekiang, Shantung, and Tientsin, which amounts to tens of thousands of taels per year.

Thus we are using the financial resources of China to fill up the bottomless hole in foreign countries.

Hard on the heels of Britain's violent prying open of China in the Opium Wars came the Indian Mutiny, also known as the Sepoy Rebellion, of 1857. This uprising came about when

Indian soldiers, called Sepoys, who had been recruited to conquer and maintain order for the British East India Company revolted. As the British expanded their foreign interests, they and most of the other powers that followed used colonized peoples in their armies and in local bureaucracies. They also hired armies of mercenaries from local princes and thereby cut the costs of running the empire. The hired armies gave the local princes revenues, while the employment of Indians to do some of the colonizers' work created a buffer between the British and the indigenous people.

Over a period of years the British East India Company had ridden roughshod over a number of Indian customs: reformers had tried to stop the burning of widows on their husband's death. The company had attacked the caste system that classified Indians into strictly regulated groups, while missionaries had encouraged Indians' conversion to Christianity. The introduction of a new rifle into the Indian army also became offensive, because soldiers had to bite the end off cartridges that had been greased with a mixture of beef and pork fat. The Sepoys rebelled because beef and pork were meats forbidden to Hindus and Muslims respectively. Although this blatant disregard for both sets of religious laws infuriated Indian soldiers, the mutiny sparked the smoldering resentments of princes and members of the middle and upper classes who were becoming increasingly outraged at the East India Company's high-handedness, favoritism, and attacks on important social customs. The widespread rebellion brought violent attacks on British soldiers and civilians alike, but the reprisals on Indians were far worse. Back home, the British government determined to end the rule of the East India Company and take direct control of India. With Queen Victoria's Proclamation to the Princes, Chiefs, and People of India (1858) of British governmental rule, the world entered a crucial stage in modern imperialism, as others joined Britain's drive for direct rule in Asia.

We hereby announce to the native princes of India that all treaties and engagements made with them by or under the authority of the Honourable East India Company are by us accepted, and will be scrupulously maintained, and we look for the like observance on their part.

We desire no extension of our present territorial possessions; and, while we will permit no aggression upon our dominions or

Opium

The opium poppy has been known for its healing properties since ancient times, and indeed 18th- and 19th-century people used it to relieve pain much as we use aspirin or ibuprofen. Unlike modern pain relievers, however, opium is highly addictive and its users often could not stop taking the substance in its many forms. Influenced by Enlightenment ideas of the crucial nature of both reason and the imagination, Europeans came to experiment with the drug in the late 18th and early 19th centuries. The scientist Sir Humphry Davy, for instance, recorded his sensations and state of mind while taking opium, and romantic writers tried to infuse their novels and poetry with intense feelings induced by it. The novelist Sir Walter Scott reported writing *Lucia di Lammermoor* under the influence of opium. Meanwhile, the Chinese used opium in public spaces designed for its consumption known as the opium den. Beginning with the Chinese, governments started clamping down on opium for leisure-time activity as well as for pain relief.

Debilitating as a habit, opium use angered the Chinese government not only because of its effect on ordinary people, but because of British coercion that the opium be admitted to China. Opium smoking became a habit among many Chinese, as the East India Company dumped thousands of pounds of the product into the country.

An Indian servant attends Queen Victoria as she reviews official documents. The queen conspicuously employed Indians as her servants in England. She relished her status as ruler of India, and loved the colony's many products, giving Indian shawls and other fancy goods as gifts.

our rights to be attempted with impunity, we shall sanction no encroachment on those of others. We shall respect the rights, dignity, and honour of native princes as our own; and we desire that they, as well as our own subjects, should enjoy that prosperity and that social advancement which can only be secured by internal peace and good government.

We hold ourselves bound to the natives of our Indian territories by the same obligations of duty which bind us to all our other subjects, and those obligations, by the blessing of Almighty God, we shall faithfully and conscientiously fulfill.

Firmly relying ourselves on the truth of Christianity, and acknowledging with gratitude the solace of religion, we disclaim alike the right and the desire to impose our convictions on any of our subjects. We declare it to be our royal will and pleasure that none be in any wise favoured, none molested or disquieted, by reason of their religious faith or observances, but that all shall alike enjoy the equal and impartial protection of the law; and we do strictly charge and enjoin all those who may be in authority under us that they abstain from all interference with the religious belief or worship of any of our subjects on pain of our highest displeasure.

And it is our further will that, so far as may be, our subjects, of whatever race or creed, be freely and impartially admitted to offices in our service, the duties of which they may be qualified by their education, ability, and integrity duly to discharge.

We know, and respect, the feelings of attachment with which natives of India regard the lands inherited by them from their ancestors, and we desire to protect them in all rights connected therewith, subject to the equitable demands of the State; and we will that generally, in framing and administering the law, due regard be paid to the ancient rights, usages, and customs of India.

Grounds for Conquest

By British logic, ruling India necessitated ruling the areas that led to it; then one had to control the areas around these routes, making for an endless list of places to conquer. Thus, the takeover of the Egyptian government in the 1880s resulted from the domination of India, which led in turn to a scramble for Africa, and indeed for the rest of the globe. Because the opening of the Suez Canal in 1869 speeded passage to India, the British saw Egypt, which controlled canal access, as even more crucial to its own prosperity.

A second reason fortified the British commitment to intervene in Egypt: they wanted to ensure that the Egyptians paid their debts to British financiers and wanted to protect England's investments in railroads, canals, dams, and agricultural enterprises there. Those debts had resulted from the modernizing efforts of Egypt's ruler Muhammad Ali (1805–48) and his successors, who took out loans from European bankers at exorbitant interest rates to gain Western technology and build a European-style army. As pasha, or chief governor, for the Ottoman sultan in Constantinople (now Istanbul), Muhammad Ali was so successful politically that he and his successors made Egypt virtually independent of the Ottoman Empire.

Once the British stepped in, Evelyn Baring, the Earl of Cromer, took charge behind the scenes of the government in Egypt. His justification for why Britain should rule this distant country, taken from his memoirs, has been called Orientalist, meaning that it used Western values to create a negative picture of other ethnicities and cultures. Besides the directly political form Orientalism can take, it is often seen to produce exoticism in the arts and in the traveler's view of foreign people. Here Lord Cromer justifies the British conquest using the most negative Orientalist arguments.

Egypt is not the only country which has been brought to the verge of ruin by a persistent neglect of economic laws and by a reckless administration of the finances of the State. Neither is it the only country in whose administration the most elementary principles of law and justice have been ignored. Although the

"It is a source of great satisfaction and pride to her to feel herself in direct communication with that enormous Empire which is so bright a jewel of her Crown, and which she would wish to see happy, contented and peaceful. May the publication of her Proclamation be the beginning of a new era and may it draw a veil over the sad and bloody past."

—Queen Victoria, on the proclamation of Britain's direct rule of India, 1858

Imperialist overseers of projects like railroads, designed to extract the region's resources as efficiently as possible, used local forced labor. Imperialist construction of harbors, roads, and railroads forever changed the landscape of conquered areas.

details may differ, there is a great similarity in the general character of the abuses which spring up under Eastern Governments wheresoever they may be situated. So also, although the remedies to be applied must vary according to local circumstances and according to the character, institutions, and habits of thought of the European nation under whose auspices reforms are initiated, the broad lines which those reforms must take are traced out by the commonplace requirements of European civilisation, and must of necessity present some identity of character, whether the scene of action be India, Algiers, Egypt, Tunis, or Bosnia.

The history of reform in Egypt, therefore, does not present any striking feature to which some analogy might not perhaps be found in other countries where European civilisation has, in a greater or less degree, been grafted on a backward Eastern Government and society. . . .

Sir Alfred Lyall [a British official and Orientalist] once said to me: "Accuracy is abhorrent to the Oriental mind. Every Anglo-Indian official should always remember that maxim." Want of accuracy, which easily degenerates into untruthfulness, is, in fact, the main characteristic of the Oriental mind.

The European is a close reasoner; his statements of fact are devoid of ambiguity; he is a natural logician, albeit he may not have studied logic; he loves symmetry in all things; he is by nature skeptical and requires proof before he can accept the truth of any proposition; his trained intelligence works like a piece of mechanism. The mind of the Oriental, on the other hand, like his picturesque streets, is eminently wanting in symmetry. His reasoning is of the most slipshod description. Although the ancient Arabs acquired in a somewhat high degree the science of dialectics [logic], their descendants are singularly deficient in the logical faculty. They are often incapable of drawing the most obvious conclusions from any simple premises of which they may admit the truth. Endeavor to elicit a plain statement of facts from an ordinary Egyptian. His explanation will generally be lengthy, and wanting in lucidity. He will probably contradict himself half-a-dozen times before he has finished his story. . . .

Or, again, look at the fulsome flattery, which the Oriental will offer to his superior and expect to receive from his inferior, and compare the general approval of such practices with the European frame of mind, which spurns both the flatterer and the person who invites flattery. This contemptible flatter . . . is, indeed, a thorn in the side of the Englishman in Egypt, for it prevents Khedives and Pashas [Egyptian rulers and officials] from hearing the truth from their own countrymen.

Europeans believed in their superiority especially to Africans, whose coastline had been dotted for centuries with European slave-trading centers. Traders from Muslim societies had also drawn slaves from Africa while working successfully to convert many of its ethnic groups. Europeans ended the slave trade in their own societies because Enlightenment thinkers saw slavery as a denial of natural rights. In addition, religious people increasingly came to see slavery as immoral. For others, growing competition among traders made conditions tense.

Although European powers and the United States individually outlawed the slave trade, it continued to be common practice among Africans, Arab traders, and the imperialists themselves. Even in the 20th century Africans were forced into work for Europeans, 100,000 of them being sent as laborers to Europe during World War I. It was called a form of conscription, but the practice was actually enslavement.

Freebooter Imperialists

Imperialists came in many varieties. The zealous late 19th-century German patriot Karl Peters wanted his country to have as great an empire as Britain's. After founding the Society for German Colonization, he gathered enough funds and equipment and a dozen men to accompany him to East Africa in the fall of 1884. There he conducted lavish ceremonials during which chiefs signed "treaties of eternal friendship" and denied any affiliation to the dominant local ruler, the sultan of Zanzibar. In 1885 Peters, a believer in ghosts, numerology, and other mystical doctrines presented these claims to some 55,000 square miles of African territory to German chancellor Otto von Bismarck. They formed the basis of Germany's claim to East Africa.

Even while the official European slave trade declined in the 19th century, the exploitation of Africa and Africans grew. Many exploratory voyages by whites to the interior showed them where to find ivory, rubber, vegetable oils, and precious metals and minerals, most notably gold and then diamonds. After the 1870s the number of explorers mounted, as did clashes and international rivalries for territory in Africa. With their industrial advantage the British had mapped out "spheres of influence" in which their trade would predominate. Then, as other countries developed industrially, they too needed the markets and raw materials the British seemed to control, the more so as a series of booms and busts tested the modernizing societies from 1873 to the turn of the century. The British takeover of Egypt in 1882 was both a threat to the other powers and a sign to take advantage of opportunities in the region. From the 1880s on, the European powers converted a relationship with Africa based on trade to one of empire based on political domination. They often did so by making treaties in which African leaders signed away rights to land and natural resources, allied themselves with the great powers or their agents to fight rivals for control, and agreed to pay the Europeans taxes and tribute.

The situation was so volatile that the powers made treaties and agreements almost daily to set boundaries and resolve other matters. In 1884–85 the great powers met in Berlin to agree upon guidelines for a parceling out of Africa that would minimize the threat of war with one another. In particular the congress established the Congo Free State, a private undertaking of King Leopold II of Belgium, who claimed to want to improve the lives of Africans in setting up this state. Until his rulership over this area was established at the congress, King Leopold had driven the explorer Henry Stanley to exhaustion in pursuit of treaties with African leaders. Run-ins with explorers from rival countries made war a perpetual threat. Thus, the congress set certain provisions for claiming an African region.

General Act of the Berlin West Africa Conference, 1885:

Art. 34: Any Power which henceforth takes possession of a tract of land on the coasts of the African continent outside of its present possessions, or which, being hitherto without such possessions, shall acquire them, as well as the Power which assumes a

Protectorate there, shall accompany the respective act with notification thereof addressed to the other Signatory Powers of the present Act, in order to enable them, if need be, to make good any claims of their own.

Art. 35: The Signatory Powers of the Present Act recognize the obligation to ensure the establishment of authority in regions occupied by them on the coasts of the African Continent sufficient to protect existing rights, and, as the case may be, freedom of trade and of transit under the conditions agreed upon. . . .

Nonetheless, the establishment of Leopold's rule in the Congo continued to bring incredible violence to the region. It was the natives who suffered from his greed and the brutality of his agents. His was not the only case where a claim of good intentions obscured a grim reality. To secure African regions, countries used armies of African slaves or free men or of paid soldiers in their conquests. Africans resisted these invasions and annexations every step of the way. In many cases the European governments also turned over the costly role of pacification and rule to their various mining, rubber, and other companies. In this document of 1886 the British government grants a charter to the National African Company that came to dominate trade in the Niger region. It gives broad powers to this private company while, like Leopold, it advertises the benefits that contact with Europeans would bring.

Victoria, by the Grace of God, of the United Kingdom of Great Britain and Ireland, Queen, Defender of the Faith. . . .

[W]hereas the Petition . . . states that the Kings, Chiefs, and peoples of various territories in the basin of the River Niger, in Africa, fully recognising after many years experience, the benefits accorded to their countries by their intercourse with the Company and their predecessors, have ceded the whole of their respective territories to the Company by various Acts of Cession [documents by which leaders surrendered their lands to imperialist agents] specified in the Schedule hereto. . . .

And whereas the Petition further states that the condition of the natives inhabiting the aforesaid territories would be materially improved, and the development of such territories and those contiguous thereto, and the civilization of their peoples would be greatly advanced if We should think fit to confer on the Company . . . Our Royal Charter. . . .

British imperialist visions, such as J. M. Gandy's plan for an imperial palace for British rulers and the government, became ever more grandiose. By the time this watercolor was painted in 1836, England had expanded to take over Scotland, Ireland, and increasing numbers of trading areas around the world.

1. The said NATIONAL AFRICAN COMPANY, LIMITED . . . is hereby authorized and empowered to hold and retain the full benefit of the several Cessions . . . and all rights, interests, authorities, and powers for the purposes of government, preservation of public order, protection of the said territories, or otherwise of what nature or kind soever. . . .

7. The Company as such, or its Officers as such, shall not in any way interfere with the religion of any class or tribe of the people of its territories, or of any of the inhabitants thereof, except so far as may be necessary in the interests of humanity. . . .

8. In the administration of Justice by the Company to the peoples of its territories, or to any of the inhabitants thereof, careful regard shall always be had to the customs and laws of the class, or tribe, or nation to which the parties respectively belong. . . .

12. The Company is hereby further authorized and empowered, subject to the approval of Our Secretary of State, to acquire and take by purchase, cession, or other lawful means, other rights, interests, authorities, or powers of any kind or nature whatever, in, over, or affecting other territories, lands, or property in the region aforesaid, and to hold, use, enjoy, and exercise the same for the purposes of the Company. . . .

14. . . . The customs duties and charges hereby authorized [that the Company shall collect] shall be levied and applied solely for the purpose of defraying the necessary expenses of government, including the administration of justice, the maintenance of order, and the performance of Treaty obligations. . . .

The Company from time to time, either periodically or otherwise, as may be directed by Our Secretary of State, shall furnish accounts and particulars in such form, and verified, in such manner as he requires, of the rates, incidence, collection, proceeds, and application of such duties. . . .

Russia, like Britain, had been colonizing for centuries, though its colonies were adjoining its frontiers, unlike the British transoceanic outposts. As Russia continued its expansion into east and central Asia by invading adjacent territories there, it annexed people of many ethnicities and religions. At one point its government explained empire building to the other great powers in terms of state security and advancing civilization. In Russian eyes, expansion was a never-ending process.

The situation of Russia in central Asia is similar to that of all civilized states that come into contact with half-savage nomadic tributes without firm social organization. In such cases, the interests of border security and trade relations always require that the more civilized state have a certain authority over its neighbors, whose wild and unruly customs render them very troublesome. It begins first by curbing raids and pillaging. To put an end to these, it is often compelled to reduce the neighboring tribes to some degree of close subordination. Once this result has been achieved, the latter take on more peaceful habits, but in turn they are exposed to the attack of tribes living farther off. . . . The state therefore must make a choice: either to give up this continuous effort and doom its borders to constant unrest, which would make prosperity, safety, and cultural progress impossible here, or else to advance farther and farther into the heart of savage lands, where the vast distances, with every step forward, increase the difficulties and hardships it incurs. Such has been the fate of all states placed in a similar situation. The United States of America, France in Africa, Holland in its colonies, England in the East Indies—they all were inevitably driven to choose the path of onward movement, not so much from ambition as from dire necessity, where the greatest difficulty lies in being able to stop.

The Far East saw not only the Russians and the English but also virtually every other big power seeking its share of territory and trade by the end of the 19th century. French expansion had started in the early modern period as France colonized parts of the Caribbean, North America, and Asia. Its army, missionaries, and traders were on the front line of this expansion, often driving government policy. In the 1830s France's trade in raw materials and small manufactured goods with Africa picked up, and it began the brutal conquest of Algeria. European settlers then flocked to claim the farmland seized from the local Algerian peoples. After the Germans defeated the French emperor Napoleon III in 1870, France became a republic ruled by an elected government. In the new climate of freedom of the press and public debate, colonial expansion became a topic of heated discussion even as traders, explorers, and the military were delving further into Africa and other continents. Shouldn't the government worry more about Germany than the remote reaches of Indochina or Africa? What was to be gained from the expense of war, bureaucracy, and settlement? Should the French be constantly fighting indigenous peoples? Here, minister of the interior and former governor of Tonkin (present-day Vietnam) Ernst Constans pleads in the French parliament for approval of funds to continue the effort of colonization in southeast Asia.

If you could see, as I have, the colonists of Haiphong and Hanoi; if you could see for yourselves the energy and ardor with which they work like mad, the conviction they muster to reach good results! Frankly you would think twice before taking part in a vote that will make these brave people believe themselves lost, them, their families and their property, if we abandon them . . . [Applause]

I know that it's not fashionable to say good things about Tonkin. I know that one needs a good deal of courage to say what one thinks; and the good things that I think of this country I will have the honor of saying here.

Messieurs, I believe that Tonkin can and must survive. I believe that it asks for nothing but to be developed and that it will develop itself if we give something of ourselves, give it a civilian administration and eliminate all its worries and all the difficulties that have been placed on it until now. I say that Tonkin can survive because I believe it to be rich. All parts along the rivers are cultivated and cultivable. No one among those who has seen Tonkin can doubt that its Delta is a great source of wealth for the country. . . .

Tonkin has been at war for ten years. All the people from the mountains have fled to the valleys to avoid either foreign attacks or rebel invasions, and they have collected in numerous villages around rivers and streams that will give them security. Thus, the Delta has become overpopulated and the mountains depopulated. But it is absolutely sure that once the Annamites [Annam was a historic kingdom in eastern Indochina] understand that they have nothing to fear from us, they will return to the lands they have abandoned, which I have visited, which are lands on which one can grow everything, and on which one will do so in the future and to great profit. . . .

I am confident that this enterprise—the colonization of Tonkin—will fully succeed; I am convinced that two years from now, you will no longer have to debate subsidies for Tonkin, which will have become self-sufficient. . . .

In any case, you cannot, my dear colleagues, fault the feelings that I express here; it is based on facts; it is also a deep conviction, I have faith that Tonkin will survive and prosper if we want it to. . . .

Newcomers Join the Race for Empire

In 1868 the Japanese instituted a new government commit- ted to modernization and development. The Meiji Restora- tion, a period so-named to mark "rebirth of enlightened rule" in Japan, involved extensive study of the West on the part of modernizers and an attempt at building an empire as the Europeans were doing. Japan saw empire as one key to Western power and also as a way to satisfy the old warrior classes, whose role had declined with the rise of industrial leaders and professionals. Korea, being a closed market where China and Russia were jockeying for control, seemed a logical point of expansion. As in the West, however, empire and the strategies leading to it were hotly contested. In 1873, soon after the Restoration, those who wanted a war of conquest in Korea were overridden by others who thought Japan unprepared as yet for such a venture. Saigō Takamori, a military leader, argues for war in a letter to a friend dated

In this French cartoon, Japan (left) and China fish in the same waters to catch Korea, while Russia watches the contest intently, its own fishing pole ready and waiting. All three powers had competing interests in East Asia, which affect international politics right down to the present day.

July 29, 1873—a communication that shows a military spirit of honor and sacrifice as well as training in diplomatic maneuvering.

Has any decision been made on Korea, now that Soejima [the foreign minister] is back? . . .

When a decision is at last reached, what will it involve if we send troops first? The Koreans will unquestionably demand their withdrawal, and a refusal on our part will lead to war. We shall then have fomented a war in a manner very different from the one you originally had in mind. Would it not be far better therefore to send an envoy first? It is clear that if we did so the Koreans would resort to violence, and would certainly afford us the excuse for attacking them.

In the event that it is decided to send troops first, difficulties may arise in the future [elsewhere]. Russia has fortified Saghalien [Sakhalin, between Russia and northern Japan] and other islands, and there have already been frequent incidents of violence. I am convinced that we should send troops to defend these places before we send them to Korea.

If it is decided to send an envoy officially, I feel sure that he will be murdered. I therefore beseech you to send me. I cannot claim to make as splendid an envoy as Soejima, but if it is a question of dying, that, I assure you, I am prepared to do.

Slowly the Japanese asserted their influence in Korea and gained control. This official document shows the Japanese government exercising the muscle that the development of its businesses and army gave it. Even though Korea was technically a sovereign state, Japanese diplomats believed they

could virtually set conditions for the functioning of the Korean government. It was only a short step to full annexation, which the Japanese accomplished in 1910 after the assassination of its resident governor in Korea.

1. The Korean Government shall pledge that they [will] adopt the administrative reform plan recommended by the Japanese Government and [will] carry it out step by step.

2. As to the construction of the railways between Seoul and Pusan and between Seoul and Inchon which is referred to in the reform plan, the Korean Government, so long as their public finance is not strong enough, shall enter into a contract with the Japanese Government or a Japanese company and start the construction of said railways. . . .

3. As to the telegraphic lines which have already been laid between Seoul and Pusan and between Seoul and Inchon by the Japanese Government, the Korean Government shall conclude a treaty . . . and shall maintain them.

4. The Korean Government shall employ Japanese on the recommendation of the Japanese Government as legal and political advisers for the execution of the Korean administrative reforms. But when these reforms have been accomplished the continued employment of those Japanese advisers shall be discussed between the two governments.

5. The . . . Japanese military instructors shall follow the provision of the preceding article.

6. In order to promote further amity and encourage commerce between the two countries, the Korean Government shall open a port for foreign trade in the province of Cholla.

Germany became a modern, unified nation-state only in 1871, when the dozens of independent territories and large kingdoms like Saxony and Bavaria joined together under the leadership of Prussia. Given their late start as a single nation, many in that country felt disadvantaged in comparison with the British and French colonization efforts that had spanned centuries. The first chancellor, Otto von Bismarck, helped Germany acquire a few colonies in order to gain the political support of traders and nationalists who saw empire as the road to grandeur. After Bismarck's dismissal in 1890, the new kaiser (emperor) William II sought colonies more aggressively. Powerful lobbies, or political pressure groups, developed to support expansionism. One of these, the Pan-German

"Every year on the anniversary of the Emperor Jimmu's accession . . . and on the anniversary of his passing . . . we should ceremonially increase the territory of the Japanese empire, even if it only be in small measure. Our naval vessels on each of these days should sail to a still unclaimed island, occupy it, and hoist the Rising Sun [the Japanese flag]."
—Shiga Shigetaka, advocate of Japanese expansion, 1890

"I would annex the planets if I could."
—Cecil Rhodes

League, presented a political rationale for world empire based on frank expressions of German racial superiority that needed to be fortified by global domination. By this time Germany had universal male suffrage, and the League helped mobilize support for the government in elections. It aimed to draw votes from working-class parties that often advocated peace and cooperation. Programs based on imperialist conquest and militant nationalism came to attract the millions of working men who now made up the electorate in an age of mass politics.

I. CONSTITUTION OF THE PAN-GERMAN LEAGUE

1. The Pan-German League strives to quicken the national sentiment of all Germans and in particular to awaken and foster the sense of racial and cultural kinship of all sections of the German people.

2. These aims imply that the Pan-German League works for:

a) Preservation of the German people in Europe and overseas and its support wherever threatened.

b) Settlement of all cultural, educational, and school problems in ways that shall aid the German people.

c) The combating of all forces which check the German national development.

d) An active policy of furthering German interests in the entire world. . . .

II. POLICIES OF THE PAN-GERMAN LEAGUE

1. Adoption of bill for reorganization of the navy.

2. Laying of a cable from Kiaochow to Port Arthur [both in China], with connection with the Russian-Siberian cable.

3. Strengthening of the German foothold in Kiaochow.

4. German coaling and cable stations in the Red Sea, the West Indies and near Singapore.

5. Complete possession of Samoa.

6. More subsidized German steamship lines to Kiaochow and Korea.

7. Understanding with France, Spain, Portugal, and the Netherlands about the laying of an independent cable from West Africa through the Congo to German East Africa, Madagascar, Batavia, and Tonkin to Kiaochow.

8. Development of harbor of Swakopmund and railroads to Windhoek [in German Southwest Africa]. . . .

10. Raising of the fund for German schools in foreign countries to 500,000 marks [from 150,000 marks], [a] division in foreign office to be created to deal with these schools; creation of pension fund for their teachers; standard German textbooks to be supplied to these schools. . . .

16. Prohibition of immigration of less worthy elements into the German Empire. . . .

22. Increase in the number of German commercial consuls in the Levant [the eastern Mediterranean], Far East, South Africa, Central and South America. . . .

The European settlers of the United States had defeated millions of the North American continent's inhabitants through warfare and disease. They then took the Native Americans' land for themselves and drove the remaining native peoples into "reservations." Although it purchased Alaska in 1867 from Russia, the new country mostly achieved its annexation of lands using the same kind of violence Europeans elsewhere did. After the Civil War, the United States began growing rich through rapid industrialization. It watched the expansion of other countries with increasing envy and distress because of the markets and sources of raw materials the great powers were coming to monopolize.

In the meantime, American missionaries and entrepreneurs had moved to islands in the Pacific, and many saw

By the mid-19th century, Americans had taken over Hawaiian land to set up sugar plantations, worked by local laborers, to feed a growing U.S. demand for sweets. Until the arrival of North Americans, Hawaiians had traded sandalwood and other products with Asia.

business opportunities in the decline of Spanish power over Cuba and other parts of its empire. Through a series of maneuvers, the monarchy of Hawaii came under the protection of the United States. But many politicians disagreed with the growing U.S. domination over the Hawaiian islands. The United States, they said, should not imitate the greedy and brutal ways of Europe. President Benjamin Harrison drew up a treaty to annex Hawaii when U.S. settlers like Sanford B. Dole, the pineapple planter, and missionaries led a coup to overthrow Queen Liliuokalani. But his successor, Grover Cleveland, withdrew the treaty. Advocates of annexation were enraged by Cleveland's move, and by 1898 popular sentiment for imperialism had gained the upper hand. In that year Hawaii was annexed and the United States defeated Spain, acquiring the Philippines in the process. Here is Harrison's justification for annexation in an 1893 message to Congress, followed by Grover Cleveland's reversal of policy.

The overthrow of the monarchy was not in any way promoted by this Government but had its origin in what seems to have been a reactionary and revolutionary policy on the part of Queen Liliuokalani, which put in serious peril not only the large and preponderating interests of the United States in the islands, but all foreign interests, and, indeed, the decent administration of civil affairs and the peace of the islands. It is quite evident that the monarchy had become effete and the Queen's Government so weak and inadequate as to be the prey of designing and unscrupulous persons. The restoration of Queen Liliuokalani to her throne is undesirable, if not impossible, and unless actively supported by the United States would be accompanied by serious disaster and the disorganization of all business interests. The influence and interest of the United States in the islands must be increased and not diminished.

Only two courses are now open—one the establishment of a protectorate by the United States, and the other annexation full and complete. I think the latter course, which has been adopted in the treaty, will be highly promotive of the best interests of the Hawaiian people, and is the only one that will adequately secure the interests of the United States. These interests are not wholly selfish. It is essential that none of the other great powers shall secure these islands. Such a possession would not consist with our safety and with the peace of the world.

When Grover Cleveland succeeded to the Presidency that same year, he withdrew the treaty. His justification to Congress reflected the kinds of doubts many had about empire.

I suppose that right and justice should determine the path to be followed in treating this subject. If national honesty is to be disregarded and a desire for territorial extension or dissatisfaction with a form of government not our own ought to regulate our conduct, I have entirely misapprehended the mission and character of our Government and the behavior which the conscience of our people demands of their public servants.

When the present Administration entered upon its duties, the Senate had under consideration a treaty providing for the annexation of the Hawaiian Islands to the territory of the United States. Surely under our Constitution and laws the enlargement of our limits is a manifestation of the highest attribute of sovereignty, and if entered upon as an Executive act all things relating to the transaction should be clear and free from suspicion. Additional importance attached to this particular treaty of annexation because it contemplated a departure from unbroken American tradition in providing for the addition to our territory of islands of the sea more than 2,000 miles removed from our nearest coast.

These considerations might not of themselves call for interference with the completion of a treaty entered upon by a previous Administration, but . . . it did not appear that [the] Provisional Government had the sanction of either popular revolution or suffrage. . . .

As I apprehend the situation, we are brought face to face with the following conditions:

The lawful Government of Hawaii was overthrown without the drawing of a sword or the firing of a shot by a process every step of which, it may safely be asserted, is directly traceable to and dependent for its success upon the agency of the United States acting through its diplomatic and naval representatives. . . .

But for the presence of the United States forces in the immediate vicinity and in position to afford all needed protection and support the committee [of planters and missionaries] would not have proclaimed the provisional government from the steps of the Government building. . . .

Believing, therefore, that the United States could not, under the circumstances disclosed, annex the islands without justly incurring the imputation of acquiring them by unjustifiable methods, I shall not again submit the treaty of annexation. . . .

Hawaiian king Kalakaua topples from his throne in this 1887 cartoon. Foreign business classes backed the king, who hoped to oust the Europeans and Americans from the Pacific and rule the region as an authoritative king once back in power. "Hawaii for the Hawaiians" was his motto.

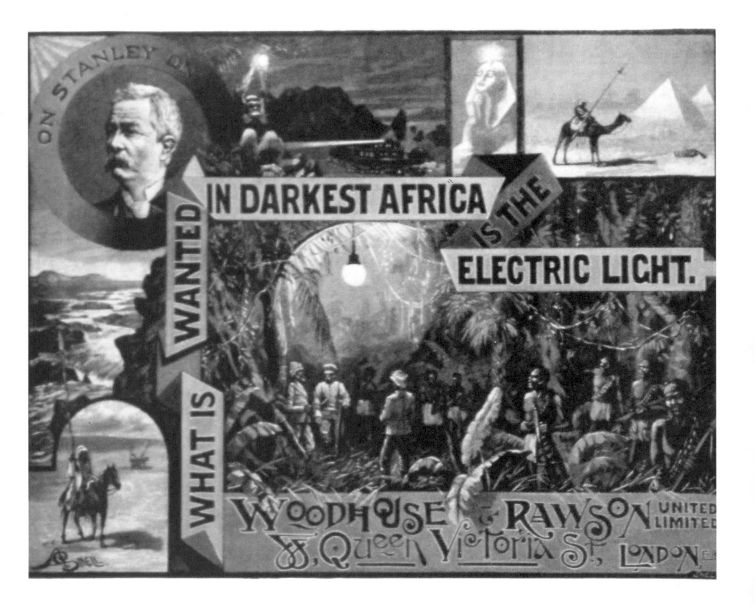

Chapter Three

Technology and Economics

In 1869 the Suez Canal opened, connecting the Mediterranean Sea to the Red Sea and thus cutting the shipping distance from Britain to India by some 40 percent, from more than 12,000 miles to about 7,000. The canal, combined with rapid advances in shipbuilding and rail transport, both chopped the cost of business and speeded it up. A trip from Europe to the Far East, which could take up to a year in the 18th century, took only two weeks in the early 20th. And the cost of transporting such goods as tea, wool, and exotic woods fell by as much as 95 percent. The results of this new technology were speed in international contacts, greater affordability of goods, and vast profits from worldwide commerce. All these changes make it accurate to call the 19th-century age of imperialism an era of a global economy achieved through technology.

Rapidly advancing industry and commerce in the early 19th century made the transformation in communications and costs possible. After 1815 and the defeat of Napoleon, the great powers of Europe generally avoided being drawn into wars over colonies and international trade for a few decades. People concentrated instead on modernizing agriculture, manufacturing, and commerce. Textile and tool-making factories sprang up; steamships and railroads began connecting industrial and commercial cities. Individual traders were making profits around the globe. These entrepreneurs were buying raw materials such as vegetable oils from Africa to use as lubrication for industrial machinery, or were carrying on a brisk export trade, taking raw materials from one distant area to another. The case of buying opium from India and reselling it to the Chinese is one striking example. The discovery of new materials seemed endless, from the vegetable oils, ivory, and rubber prominent before midcentury to the diamonds, gold, and petroleum of later years.

The push to the interior of Africa and Asia occurred with the modernization of industry and transport as steamships and railroads changed the landscape of the colonies too. By the early 19th century, traders had saturated the coastal areas of continental Asia and Africa. As industry grew, businessmen increased their efforts to push into the interior to defeat the competition by

Imperialism sold! An advertisement relies on the romance of the Sphinx and the pyramids, the exoticism of African natives, and the bravery of explorer Henry Morton Stanley. Its tagline appealed to whites' sense of superiority: People without modern products were backward, like natives, whereas those with them were nobler, fit, and enlightened.

finding untapped markets and untouched sources of raw materials. At the same time, the push to the interior was itself part of the spread of railroads and steamships to those areas as financiers learned that there was money to be made in building railroads and making other investments in non-Western lands. The development of such costly enterprises to start up and run as mining, transportation systems, and ultimately oil refineries also provided opportunity for profit. The money invested in railroads and telegraph lines and cables could only enhance profitability, however, if local governments provided protection. For instance, the British companies building railroads in India did not have to worry about efficiency, because the British government promised the mostly British investors a 5 percent return on their money. When huge cost overruns ate into profits, the government made up the shortfall in profits by increasing Indian taxes.

Newly developed large plantations and mines also needed government protection from political resistance by those forced to work on them. Potential sites for imperial investment—in agriculture, mining, and other wealth-creating enterprises—needed to be pacified and then reorganized for that economic activity to take place. In fact, as imperial entrepreneurs muscled their way into traditional routes of trade and upset local economies and ways of life, and as settlers wrested land from those who controlled it, violence escalated. It is a superiority in arms, even warfare waged by well-trained imperial armies, that is usually said to have made the imperial seizure of land and resources possible. Indeed, the Europeans and Japanese rapidly industrialized not only around textiles and railroads but around the manufacture of modern weaponry, such as machine guns, and the development of colonial armed forces.

What made the difference is the modern nation-state's mobilization of arms, armies, and other trained personnel. Asians and Africans had access to arms too, although unscrupulous traders

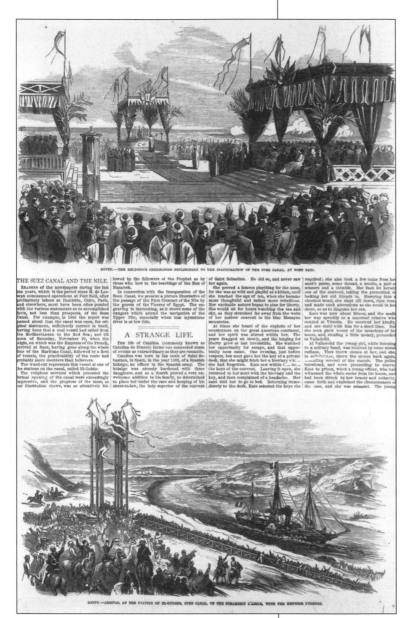

The opening of the Suez Canal in 1869 caused great celebration and advanced imperialism because it allowed more rapid passage to the resources and markets of Asia. Planned by the French engineer Ferdinand de Lesseps, the Suez Canal cost the lives of thousands of Egyptians and quickly came to be dominated by the European powers.

often sold them inferior models or rejects. However, the nation-wide system of centralized military organization that Europeans and the Japanese developed provided training in the use of arms, the benefit of a regular officer corps, an army corps of engineers for building roads, canals, and harbors, and an increasingly nation-alistic camaraderie among all types of adventurer-businessmen and government officials.

The modern nation-state made the decision to put its central-ized power in the field to protect the investments of its citizens. In contrast, those who attempted to resist the imperialists came from a variety of ethnic groups with varying and even competing loyal-ties. Possessing guns merely encouraged them to fight pitched bat-tles in which European military organization held the advantage. More effective was the ceaseless guerrilla warfare that undefeated peoples learned to wage against their would-be rulers. Although military leaders and politicians like to mark out definite beginnings and ends to colonial wars, many historians believe that in fact, under imperialism war never stopped and peace never came.

Economic hardship often accompanied the armed violence of imperialism. Many local peoples in the 19th century were already working hard enough for their regional traders, who supplied both the growing international markets and the local ones. In Africa, the aggressive trade that grew up under imperialism made the native traders more oppressive too, causing whole tribes to migrate in search of new trading opportunities or to escape. Many people were enslaved to provide raw materials that imperialists wanted or to serve in armies to fight them off. In India, people's land was taken from them and the former farmers forced to work growing indigo, rice, or some other assigned crop, which the British then bought from them at starvation prices. These trends did not affect all colonized peoples: sometimes merchants and industrialists among them found opportunities to make vast fortunes from the new system. A very few built steel mills or invested in railroads. More generally, however, imperialism disrupted local agriculture and craft-based societies, and the rulers imposed taxes that made people leave their traditional modes of self-sufficient farming in which they could grow multiple crops that would provide all their family's needs. To get cash to pay the new imperial taxes, they moved into wage labor on plantations or in mines. Migration, constant warfare, the vio-lent appropriation of land, and the economic

Egyptomania

When Napoleon invaded Egypt in 1798–99, he was accompanied by engineers and artists who sketched Egyptian monuments, studied construction techniques, and helped determine which monuments and works of art to take back to France. This influenced the decoration of furniture, fash-ion, and cityscapes with Egyptian motifs like obelisks, pyramids, sphinxes, and palms—one of the first modern displays of Egyptomania, or the passion for Egyptian culture.

One example of Egyptomania carried in American pockets is the U.S. dollar bill, one side of which is engraved with a pyramid.

N°. I. SPINNING FINE YARN.

An illustration from a book on Indian textiles illustrates the first process in making muslin cloth in Dacca (now the capital of Bangladesh). The city's muslins were world renowned in the middle of the 19th century, but the British had destroyed the industry by the end of the century through intense competition and legal restrictions on manufacturing.

struggle of those in traditional craft work added to the hardships imperialism brought.

Ultimately, imperialists' substitution of large-scale one-crop farming of commodities that would bring large sums of money on the international market for the more balanced farming of traditional peoples is said to have done long-term ecological damage to whole continents such as Africa. The final story of imperial economics and technology is an uneven one involving opportunity and vast fortunes for some, drastic economic and technological change around the world, and real suffering for millions of people.

Plotting Profit-Making

The progress of industry that occurred among the imperial powers in the 19th century did not mean that that progress would spread to the colonies. In fact, quite the reverse was often true. In the early days of colonization, for example, Indian textiles were among the finest in the world, and European traders in the 18th century had done a thriving business in Indian chintzes and muslins. These cotton fabrics inspired a desire for their lively patterns and lightweight airiness during warm seasons, and in cooler ones Europeans' new-found taste for them in preference to their traditional woolen garments was a motivating factor in the inventions associated with the industrial revolution. Consumers snapped up the fine, delightful cotton products as fast as they could be produced, encouraging further industrialization.

Once the cheaper factory-produced English cottons were available in both Europe and India, Indian handloom workers were thrown out of business (as were their European counterparts). Within 50 years an entire sector of the Indian economy was destroyed. But when Indian modernizers tried to industrialize textiles in their turn, lobbying by English industrialists kept import taxes prohibitively high on supplies of Egyptian and American cotton to India, to retard widespread Indian success in the industry. From being leading producers of textiles, Indians became forced to import from Britain cottons they had once made themselves. Thus colonialism advanced British wealth; it accomplished this by using the strong arm of the government to dismantle Indian manufacturing and industry. Here is an official's report to the British parliament in 1840.

Indian cotton manufactures have been to a great extent displaced by English manufactures. The peculiar kind of silky cotton formerly grown in Bengal, from which the fine Dacca muslins used to be made, is hardly ever seen; the population of the town of Dacca has fallen from 150,000 to 30,000 or 40,000 and the jungle and malaria are fast encroaching upon the town. The only cotton manufactures which stand their ground in India are the very coarse kinds, and the English cotton manufactures are generally consumed by all above the very poorest throughout India. . . . Dacca which was the Manchester of India, has fallen off from a very flourishing town to a very poor and small one; the distress there has been very great indeed.

Imperialists had in mind that colonized peoples in tropical regions would buy their products and provide them with food, minerals, and other raw materials—not compete with them in industry. Vast plantations for crop production took shape, while scientists from imperializing countries worked to improve plant strains and discover new agricultural techniques. In the 19th and 20th centuries, botanical gardens flourished as never before, only now their purpose was to devise ways of changing colonized peoples' agricultural practices, not to learn from them. Late in the 19th century, the British director of the Peradeniya Botanic Gardens in Sri Lanka explained the purpose of his work and the way he envisioned that colonial peoples' agriculture had to change.

The great development of European planting enterprise in more civilised and opened-up countries has of course quite revolutionised the primitive agriculture or rather has built up a modern agriculture beside it. . . . Whether planting in the tropics will always continue to be under European management is another question, but the northern powers will not permit that the rich and as yet comparatively undeveloped countries of the tropics should be entirely wasted by being devoted merely to the supply of the food and clothing wants of their own people, when they can also supply the wants of the colder zones in so many indispensable products.

Companies with rights to trade with and govern a region regularly used violent means to extract raw materials from local people under their jurisdiction. The Congo Free State

Relegated to working exclusively with handlooms, weavers in colonized regions such as Kashmir (the region for which cashmere is named) symbolized technological backwardness, whereas their products stood for luxury and high quality.

Jamsetji Tata: An Industrial Pioneer in India

The son of a wealthy cotton merchant, the late–19th-century industrialist Jamsetji Tata used his profits from global trading and his knowledge of the textile industry learned in Manchester, England, to devise ways around the difficulties of establishing a textile factory. His great success in textiles led him into iron and steel and finally into hydroelectric power. Tata set up model communities with schools, hospitals, and sports facilities for his employees. "To my father, the hydro-electric project was not merely a dividend-earning scheme," his son reported. "It was a means to an end— the development of the manufacturing power of Bombay. . . . [T]he great sums of money needed were forthcoming mainly because those who commanded them believed that the scheme would assuredly play an important part in the industrial renaissance of India."

was renowned for its brutality in the pursuit of wealth, but all countries used forced and even slave labor to make money. In the 1840s the vulcanization of rubber (a process that made the substance more stable regardless of heat and cold) converted it into a vital commodity with a vast number of industrial uses—from making waterproof clothing to serving as parts in industrial machinery. Here an American missionary describes how the collection of rubber was enforced in Belgian king Leopold's private state of the Congo.

Each town in the district is forced to bring a certain quantity [of rubber] to the headquarters of the commissaire [agent] every Sunday. It is collected by force. The soldiers drive the people into the bush. If they will not go they are shot down, and their left hands cut off and taken as trophies to the commissaire. . . . The commissaire is paid a commission of about 1d. a pound upon all the rubber he gets. It is therefore to his interest to get as much as he can. . . .

Let me give an incident to show how this unrighteous trade affects the people. One day a State corporal, who was in charge of the post of Lolifa, was going round the town collecting rubber. Meeting a poor woman whose husband was away fishing, he said, "Where is your husband?" She answered by pointing to the river. He then said, "Where is his rubber?" She answered, "It is ready for you," whereupon he said, "You lie," and, lifting his gun, shot her dead. Shortly afterwards the husband returned, and was told of the murder of his wife. He went straight to the corporal, taking with him his rubber, and asked why he had shot his wife. The wretched man then raised his gun and killed the corporal. The soldiers ran away to the headquarters of the State and made misrepresentations of the case, with the result that the commissaire sent a large force to support the authority of the soldiers; the town was looted, burned, and many people killed and wounded. . . .

Many economists who were in favor of trade and of opening markets nonetheless felt that colonization went against sound economics and was more costly than profitable. Charles Gide, a French economist and legal scholar, here summarizes the disadvantages that many of his peers foresaw.

If we consider particularly the case of France, the arguments of the adversaries of a colonial policy take on a special force; and of the three advantages which we have outlined [an outlet for emigration, profitable investments for capital, and commercial opportunity] not one remains viable.

First, regarding emigration, France has no one to spare. Its population is sparse and grows so slowly that it is only foreign immigration that will fill the country.

If France has no emigrants to send outside the country, it also has no merchandise to export. French industry specializes in making expensive and high quality, even luxury goods. It is not for selling to the Indochinese who live on a fistful of rice, nor for the Blacks in the Congo who dress in a swatch of cotton cloth that the French make Parisian luxury items, Lyon silk, or Bordeaux wine. In founding colonies in barbarian territories, France simply sets up markets for its English and German rivals.

It is true that France has abundant capital and it seems that we might profit in this way from colonies. But French capital hasn't the boldness and energy of English capital that distributes itself around the world. French capital is wealth made from modest savings and like its owners is distrustful and sparing; its timid spirit hardly leads it to invest elsewhere in Europe; and it is even more unusual for it to cross the Mediterranean to seek its fortune in Algeria, Tunisia or Egypt. . . . Let French capital remain in France; it will find plenty of opportunity.

The profit that the inhabitants of a country might make from founding colonies thus appears uncertain; the profit that the State could make appears even more problematic.

Is it the idea of dividends coming into the Treasury? This is the goal that states pursue when setting up colonies, but experience teaches them that this is a mirage. Everywhere it is the metropole that pays dividends [tribute] to its colonies.

As traders from the Lipton, Tetley, Twining, and other families demanded vast quantities of tea, plantations employing children, like these in Ceylon, spread across Asia. Imperialism changed patterns of work and family life, while it reshaped the economies of colonized peoples.

Voices of Opportunity

Colonial exploitation was never complete, nor did all colonized peoples object to it. To the contrary, some rare native peoples whose countries were occupied found in it opportunities for themselves. Mary Seacole, the daughter of a free black mother and a Scottish father, grew up among the military who secured colonized islands like Jamaica. She used

the commercial and medical skills (especially in treating tropical diseases and sicknesses such as cholera) she had learned from her mother to support herself as she traveled to different parts of the British Empire, North America, and Europe. *The Wonderful Adventures of Mrs. Seacole in Many Lands,* her unique autobiography, became a bestseller when it was published in 1857 in Britain, for it showed Mrs. Seacole ministering (like the contemporary heroine Florence Nightingale) to sick and wounded British soldiers in the Crimean War—a conflict fought over influence in the declining Ottoman Empire. The British could interpret her as the noble fruit of British colonization, but it is clear that Mrs. Seacole was also making a living in nursing and trading with the army.

How slowly and gradually I succeeded in life, need not be told at length. . . . Sometimes I was rich one day, and poor the next. I never thought too exclusively of money, believing rather that we were born to be happy, and that the surest way to be wretched is to prize it over-much. Had I done so, I should have mourned over many a promising speculation proving a failure . . . ; and perhaps lost my mind when the great fire of 1843, which devastated Kingston, burned down my poor home [a boardinghouse]. . . . But, of course, I . . . rebuilt my house by degrees, and restocked it, succeeding better than before; for I had gained a reputation as a skilful nurse and doctress, and my house was always full of invalid officers and their wives. . . . Sometimes I had a naval or military surgeon under my roof, from whom I never failed to glean instruction. . . .

[In 1850] my brother had left Kingston for the Isthmus of Panama. . . . Ever since he had done so, I had found some difficulty in checking my reviving disposition to roam, and at last persuading myself that I might be of use to him . . . I allowed no grass to grow beneath my feet, but set to work busily. . . . My house was full for weeks, of tailors, making up rough coats, trousers, etc., and sempstresses cutting out and making shirts. In addition to these, my kitchen was filled with busy people, manufacturing preserves, guava jelly, and other delicacies, while a considerable sum was invested in the purchase of preserved meats, vegetables, and eggs. . . .

Before the passengers for Panama had been many days gone, it was found that they had left one of their number behind them, and that one—the cholera. I believe that the faculty have not yet

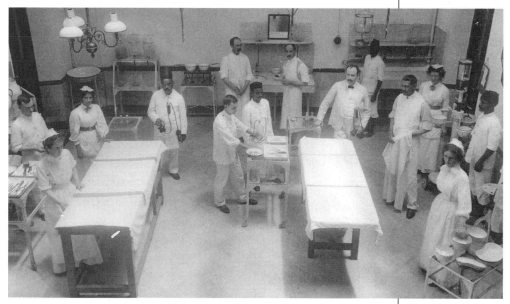

Western medical practice appealed to many Asians and Africans. It offered new job opportunities and an improved standard of living for some. Doctors and nurses in western-style hospitals were part of a colonized middle class, and many of them helped start movements to liberate their people from the imperialists' grip.

come to the conclusion that the cholera is contagious . . . but my people have always considered it to be so.

There was no doctor in Cruces [on the Isthmus of Panama] . . . and I was obliged to do my best. Selecting from my medicine chest—I never travel anywhere without it—what I deemed necessary, I went hastily to the patient, and at once adopted the remedies I considered fit. It was a very obstinate case, but by dint of mustard emetics [a substance to make a person vomit], warm fomentations, mustard plasters on the stomach and the back, and calomel, at first in large then in gradually smaller doses, I succeeded in saving my first cholera patient in Cruces. . . .

[In 1854] before I left Jamaica . . . war had been declared against Russia, and we were all anxiously expecting news of a descent upon the Crimea. Now, no sooner had I heard of war somewhere, than I longed to witness it; and when I was told that many of the regiments I had known so well in Jamaica had left England for the scene of action, the desire to join them became stronger than ever. I used to stand for hours in silent thought before an old map of the world, in a little corner of which some one had chalked a red cross, to enable me to distinguish where the Crimea was. . . .

Mrs. Seacole travels to England and finally arrives in the Crimea, where war is raging.

Before very long I found myself surrounded with patients of my own, and this for two simple reasons. In the first place, the men

The Crimean War (1853–56) provided not only an opportunity for Europeans to encroach upon the weakening Ottoman Empire, but also a chance for adventurous women such as nurse Florence Nightingale, pictured here, to travel and work. Massive casualties of wounded and ill mounted during the war.

(I am speaking of the "ranks" now) had very serious objection to going into hospital for any but urgent reasons, and the regimental doctors were rather fond of sending them there; and, in the second place, they could and did get at my store sick-comforts and nourishing food, which the heads of the medical staff would sometimes find it difficult to procure. These reasons, with the additional one that I was very familiar with the diseases which they suffered most from and successful in their treatment (I say this in no spirit of vanity), were quite sufficient to account for the numbers who came daily to the British Hotel for medical treatment.

That the officers were glad of me as a doctress and nurse may be easily understood. When a poor fellow lay sickening in his cheerless hut and sent down to me, he knew very well that I should not ride up in answer to his message empty-handed. And although I did not hesitate to charge him with the value of the necessaries I took him, still he was thankful enough to be able to *purchase* them. When we lie ill at home surrounded with comfort, we never think of feeling any special gratitude for the sick-room delicacies which we accept as a consequence of our illness; but the poor officer lying ill and weary in his cheerless hut, dependent for the merest necessaries of existence upon a clumsy, ignorant soldier-cook . . . often finds his greatest troubles in the want of those little delicacies with which a weak stomach must be humoured into retaining nourishment.

Some Asians and Africans came to admire various institutions—the highly trained armies, for example—of the colonizers, and technology drew their attention too. Trains, moving with no visible sources of power, were a source of mystery to many. During the Indian Mutiny of 1857, a rebel force surrounded a locomotive but did not dare get close, preferring instead to attack it with stones. Puzzling and even seen as a source of evil, technology was an inescapable part

of being colonized, as railroads, steamships, weapons, electricity, cameras, and ultimately radio and film moved in with the imperialists.

Colonized peoples in the middle and upper classes held a range of views about the value of such technology, some embracing it wholeheartedly, some rejecting it outright, others choosing varying degrees of acceptance and rejection. In the face of Western power, it was not hard for colonized peoples to see technology as one source of that power and to want it for themselves. People who thought this way sent their children to the European-style schools that were growing up in the colonies or even to Europe itself for an education. Some held the belief, as this Javanese leader expressed to the Dutch colonizers of his island, that technology would make people more equal and respectful of one another.

[Open up opportunities] for the sons of Java so that energies will not be dissipated, energies which could have rendered the country a service. . . . We feel it, we are aware of it, we need, besides rice and dried fish, also food for thinking people. . . . We see coaches running without horses over iron tracks; we see boats making their way through the ocean without sails; we see light that has not been kindled; we see many things which for us are only miracles and mysteries. . . . Let us join hands and let us work unceasingly for our common interests. . . . And I see the dawn of a future when, on cool evenings in the moonlight, the Javanese, accompanied by the lovely sounds of the gamelan, will send up songs of praise and gratitude in honour of his white brother.

In order to pay taxes and other charges imposed by imperial powers, colonized farmers such as these Indonesians stopped working their own lands and began working for plantation owners.

News of imperial opportunity heated up with each successive conquest and likewise circulated among the middle classes of the imperial powers. Missionaries, explorers, cartographers, and traders sent letters back from their travels. This report from a French merchant in Tonkin lists investment possibilities based on the argument that the Tonkinese were backward in extracting and refining raw materials. The author appeals to the enterprising European's sense of pride in practical know-how.

From an industrial perspective, there is much to be done, and capital is sure not to stagnate here. Things happen in this good Annam that are hallowed by routine and that are of a nature to jolt the industrialist who has some money. You would not believe that *cotton* grown here then goes to China to be spun and then returns to Tonkin where the inhabitants weave it and make it into clothing. If a spinning factory were built, it would economize on the roundtrip to China as well as on the difference between the cost of Chinese workers and Tonkinois, who are less well-paid.—*Rice* is badly processed by primitive machines, turned by hand. It thus cannot sell advantageously on Far Eastern markets.—*Sugar cane* is processed in the most incredible machines, still driven by buffaloes; what waste, what losses, what an inferior sugar results!—As for *silk,* it is even worse. Everything needs to be done; but what a huge operation, and yet so little profitable! The raw silk of Tonkin is now very defective and the spinning processes infantile. What improvements there are to make and what profits the slightest efforts would bring over the long term.

Devastation

When it came to work life in colonized areas, technology and economics usually brought about the devastation of an older way of life as plantation labor replaced the family farm, and new colonial taxes forced rural people to work on imperialists' projects like railroad building instead of remaining self-sufficient farmers. In the last third of the century, as natural resources like diamonds, gold, and ores were discovered in Africa, able-bodied men sought employment in mining or were coerced, and sometimes enslaved, to work in the mines.

Although the prospect of putting together enough money to marry (called the bride price) was another reason to work in the mines, workers soon found them horrendous, and often dangerous, places to work. Most of the major mines in the Belgian Congo and South Africa were owned by Europeans or their descendants, whose disregard for decent living and working conditions killed off huge numbers of workers. At a time when industrial countries were coming to have some concern for the well-being of their workers descended from "imperial" stock, the belief that colonized peoples were inferior resulted in a total disregard for their lives, let alone their health and comfort. Here are descriptions from two miners who left the mining camps in the Belgian Congo in the first decades of the 20th century. By this time publicity about the horrid conditions in the Congo had forced its cession from the royal family to Belgian control, but without even the minimal protection given the working classes in Europe, exploitation remained rampant and loss of life extreme.

Bwana Asani Rajabo: The drill holes chosen to hold the explosives were dug by the African foreman with a borer. It was then necessary to insert the necessary number of charges before lighting the fuse; but since the workers often miscounted the charges, they sometimes set them off before everyone had left the scene and taken shelter. That explains why we had a number of accidents at Ruashi.

We had two work crews: on one week the first worked from 7 A.M. to 3 P.M., the second from 3 P.M. to 11 P.M.; the following week the morning crew worked at night and the evening crew in the morning. No, there was no rest period and we had nothing to eat on the job. Only those who worked [underground] at Kipushi received a roll called a "kampopo" before descending into the pit.

Bwana Lungumbu Saidi: Life at the camp was pleasant; only the food did not suit us. . . . The people from Maniema died in large numbers, because they were not accustomed to maize flour. Yes, we lost many of our people at Ruashi, some died from work accidents, others, the majority, from diarrhea. The man who had diarrhea one day died in two or three days. All of us wanted only one thing: to terminate our contract and return to our country—we were so frightened by the number of people who died each day.

Imperialism wreaked havoc on traditional patterns of agriculture, trade, and manufacture, and also produced environmental devastation. Empires have long inflicted ecological

It's likely that these African miners migrated a long distance to work in a South African diamond mine. Once migrant workers arrived, Europeans forced them to remain in the mining compounds.

damage: the ancient Greek empire deforested Sicily to build its fleet of ships, with effects that remain apparent to this day in rocky terrain where for centuries it has been difficult to eke out an existence in agriculture. Before the peak of British global power the rulers of Burma (now called Myanmar) worked to balance the economies of a dry area in the highlands with the moister, food-producing economy of the delta area. The great powers were interested in that country because of its products such as precious metals and stones, teak, and pottery, its proximity to India, and its location on trade routes. As a result, the British fought a series of wars in the 19th century, and in 1862 annexed lower Burma. The government was confined to the dry north. To gain revenues it leased the forests to the Bombay-Burma Trading Company (BBTC), which stripped them of teak. Drought, famine, banditry, and general disarray ensued after only a couple of decades. When the Burmese tried to gain some compensation for this damage, the British attacked and annexed the rest of the country in the 1880s.

In 1875 British officials already knew the likely outcome of their leases to the BBTC, as their reports back home show.

The teak forest at Burmese Toungoo . . . will be worked steadily for another six or seven years, by which time it will be probably completely exhausted. Some four or five lacs [a lac was 100,000] of logs have already been extracted . . . , and 26,000 logs are now ready for removal and export. With no system of conservation, this forest must be exhausted before long.

Another official wrote:

Vague, undefined leases of vast forests cause very great destruction and waste of valuable timber. Experience has shown that lessees of this type, or their agents, destroy forests, put a stop to natural reproduction, prevent conservation or reproduction of forest resources, and denude the country to its great and lasting loss.

The Burmese administration tried to fine the BBTC for its practices, especially the felling of young trees that could have replenished the forest, but the company responded:

The Corporation have never desired to fell under-sized timber, and their own forest rules especially forbid it. . . . The Corporation were forced [to] owing to . . . another timber merchant, who offered to pay . . . a large sum for the right of felling and removing under-sized timber in the forests leased by the Corporation. Up to that period the Corporation had never consented to any small timber being felled in their forest.

While King Thebaw and his officials sought French guns and other support as the economy declined and crime and other social disorder erupted, the British officials judged that Upper Burma did not deserve its independence:

[The country] is rapidly becoming a source of danger to us instead of merely an annoyance. . . . It has degenerated in power and resources, and is unable to . . . resist the pressure and temptation of the French or other [European] influences. . . . We clearly recognize the expediency of putting an end to it. If, therefore, King Thebaw should give us legitimate provocation, it would probably be for our interest to annex the country. . . .

Imperial expansion, including the annexation of Burma, was accomplished through conquest, which depended on having an advantage in weaponry, transportation systems, and centralized organization of troops. Many troops consisted of soldiers from the colonies, but the units themselves were generally commanded by officers from the imperial power. The local resisters did not simply disappear in the face of these onslaughts, however, but in many cases devised guerrilla tactics, often maintaining their resistance for years. Native African leaders bought weapons from traders, and some set up their own facilities for producing guns.

Warfare for imperial conquest was made into a drama of technological and moral supremacy for the populations back home through memoirs, histories, novels, and reporting in the new mass journalism. Winston Churchill, who would lead Britain as prime minister during World War II, participated in campaigns in India and Africa, sending home vivid descriptions of battle such as this one at Khartoum in 1898 during which the Mahdi regime was defeated.

I have tried to draw you some picture of the advance of the army. A long row of great brown masses of infantry with a fringe of cavalry dotting the plain for miles in front, with the Camel Corps—chocolate-coloured men on cream-coloured camels—stretching

The Gatling gun was a prototype of a modern machine gun, employed first in the U.S. Civil War but soon adapted for colonial warfare. Before there were tanks, a camel served as a mount in desert warfare. The gun inflicted horrendous numbers of casualties with little personal combat, leading its victims to believe that imperialists were barbarians without a sense of military honor.

into the desert on the right and the gunboats stealing silently up river on the left, scrutinising the banks with their guns; while far behind the transport and baggage trailed away into the mirage, and far in front the telescope might discover the watching Dervish [the enemy] patrols. . . . [T]he telegraph has already told you that tremendous events that have taken place . . . [but] let me . . . describe the reconnaissance of Kerreri and the Battle of Khartoum which followed. . . .

At first nothing was apparent except the walls and houses of Amdurman and the sandy plain sloping up from the river to the distant hills. Then four miles away, on our right front, I perceived a long black line with white spots. It was the enemy. It seemed to me as we looked that there might be three thousand men behind a high dense zareba [stockade] of thorn bushes. . . .

It was made of men not bushes. Behind it other immense masses and lines of men appeared over the crest, and while we watched, amazed by the wonder of the sight, the whole of the slope became black with swarming savages. . . .

At quarter to two the Dervish army halted. . . . No sooner had they halted than their riflemen discharged their rifles in the air with a great roar—a barbaric *feu-de-joie* [bonfire]. Then they all lay down on the ground, and it became evident that the matter would not be settled till the morrow.

[Meanwhile] at about eleven o'clock the gunboats had ascended the Nile and engaged the enemy's batteries on the river face of Omdurman. Throughout the day the loud reports of their guns could be heard, and looking from our position on the ridge we could see the white vessels steaming slowly forward against the current under clouds of black smoke from their furnaces, and amid other clouds of white smoke from their artillery.

When the gunboats had completed their bombardment, had sunk a Dervish steamer, had silenced all the hostile batteries, and had sorely battered the Mahdi's Tomb, they returned leisurely to the camp and lay moored close to the bank to lend the assistance of their guns in case of attack. And as the darkness became complete they threw their powerful searchlights over the plain and on to the distant hills, and all night long these dazzling beams disturbed, though they protected, the slumbers of the army. . . .

As it became broad daylight . . . I suddenly realized that all the masses were in motion and advancing swiftly. Their Emirs galloped about, among and before their ranks scouts and patrols began to scatter themselves all over the front. Then they began to cheer.

The attack developed. . . . Forthwith the gunboats, and the 32nd Battery, and other guns from the zareba opened on them. I was but three hundred yards away, and with excellent [field] glasses could almost see the faces of the Dervishes who met the fearful fire. About twenty shells struck them in the first minute. Some burst high in the air, others exactly in their faces. Others again plunged into the sand and exploding, dashed clouds of red dust, splinters, and bullets amid their ranks. The white flags toppled over in all directions. Yet they rose again immediately, as other men pressed forward to die for Allah's sacred cause and in the defense of the successor of the True Prophet of The Only God. It was a terrible sight, for as yet they had not hurt us at all, and it seemed an unfair advantage to strike thus cruelly when they could not reply.

The enemy surrendered and soon individuals were giving up their guns, Churchill reported:

These were savages who had for many years afflicted the Sudan and cumbered the earth. We well knew the mercy they would have offered us had the fortunes of the day been reversed. . . . And there were some who would have said, "Take up your arms and fight, for there is no mercy here."

Yet it seems that those who use the powerful weapons of civilisation—the shrapnel shell, the magazine rifle, and the Maxim gun—can afford to bear all that the wild spearman may do without descending to retaliation.

The Clash of Scientific Cultures

Because conquering and maintaining an empire involved military activity, conquerors like Napoleon in Egypt set up hospitals almost immediately to keep their troops in the best health possible. Tropical diseases, along with battle wounds, attacked these soldiers, causing medical men and scientists to look for cures for malaria and yellow fever. The development of quinine in the mid–19th century as a remedy for malaria thus facilitated conquest, allowing deeper penetration of the tropical interior.

Medicine in the colonies soon played its part in the development of imperial rule. Europeans had been spreading

Tattooing

Besides participating in imperial conquest, soldiers and sailors advanced cultural exchange by bringing new practices back to their home countries. Tattooing-which uses a needle and dyes to decorate the body—was one of these practices. For thousands of years people around the globe have employed all sorts of body art to decorate themselves, to provide protection from evil forces, or to suggest their identity. Judeo-Christian prohibitions, however, made tattooing fall out of favor in the West, though the Romans, for instance, had been expert self-decorators. Empire and global trade brought sailors and soldiers into contact with body art of people in Africa and the Pacific region-indeed the word "tattoo" is of Polynesian origin. The 19th century saw a rebirth of tattooing in the West, and as global contact increases the intricate decoration of the body practiced in places like Japan has become more popular.

illness wherever they went since the beginnings of expansion, and it was no different in the 19th century, as syphilis, measles, and smallpox—to name just a few—accompanied the conquerors with devastating effect. But the imperialists attributed the weakened condition of Africans and Asians to their own poor hygiene and saw European medical science as a boon the conquered people would appreciate. "Natives returning healed to their tribes," one French doctor in Algeria declared, "would become links in a chain of sympathy invisibly binding the vanquished to the victor."

Doctors in many colonized regions used their status as colonial professionals to invade people's houses, force them to be vaccinated against smallpox, and completely rebuild (or destroy) local villages according to the outsiders' ideas of hygienic practices. Here one French doctor describes his treatment of smallpox in Algeria in 1854.

An epidemic of smallpox raged in the Beni-Slyem which I had just visited two days ago, at which time there were already eight dead. My arrival seemed to have a good effect on these terrified victims of this cruel sickness which they thought to stop by enclosing the victims, abandoning them, and forbidding them to cross certain limits. On entering each house one was stopped, suffocated by the repulsive odor. Could it be otherwise with seven or eight sick people covered with pustules and sores oozing pus, some seated, covered with their robes so as not to be devoured by the millions of flies. Each building was a hothouse of infection, some were closed up, the owners thinking to save themselves and no doubt carrying with them to other tribes the smallpox germs.

In presence of this plague, I could not think about vaccines, which took too long. . . . I made all leave their houses (it was July) and go under the shade of the big olive trees that surrounded the village while waiting for the tents that the Commandant was going to bring and place at the top of the mountain.

Then I ordered fires started at intervals in the village, aromatic herbs burned in each of the empty houses, and the washing of all clothes. . . .

Fifty years later, doctors continued to find colonized peoples "exceedingly exasperating," as one based in Uganda put it. They may have been found exasperating because some of these people had diseases doctors could not understand,

because they did not have symptoms recognizable in the West, or because they did not answer questions according to Western ways of talking about illnesses. In 1900 this doctor recorded medical encounters as taking place between an intelligent Western doctor and a ridiculous native.

Doctor: What is the matter with you?

Patient: My name is so and so.

Doctor: Yes, but what is your disease?

Patient: I want medicine to drink.

Doctor: Where do you hurt?

Patience: I don't want medicine to swallow, but to drink.

Doctor (sternly): WHAT IS YOUR ILLNESS?

Patient: Oh, it goes all over me, it cries out "Ka, ka." Will you listen to the top of my head with your hearing machine (stethoscope), etc. etc.?

As a result of these attitudes, imperialist doctors often brusquely dismissed colonized peoples' illnesses, leading the latter to utilize a variety of therapies, including herbalism, acupuncture, shiatsu (a Japanese treatment based on applying pressure to various points on the body), and local traditional cures. Distrusting the doctors, many still wanted Western medicine. When a British doctor in Lagos, Nigeria, released a series of local patients from his hospital in 1888 because he could not understand their illnesses, their subsequent deaths provoked a petition to the British authorities:

We seize this opportunity of representing seriously to your Lordship, the urgent necessity of the granting to this colony and appointing thereto, qualified native medical doctors who have graduated in Europe as Assistant Colonial Surgeons in view of what has occurred in the Colonial Hospital which is proof conclusive of that absence of feeling that should be between doctor and patient. In other West African colonies, the post of Assistant Colonial Surgeon is filled by natives. To such extent is this absence of feeling on the part of the colonial surgeons exemplified that Hausas [a native ethnic group], Policemen, native Government officials, and even convicts have avoided going and expressed refusal to go to Colonial Hospital in times of sickness, preferring native medical treatment or death at home.

Chapter Four

Imperial Societies

The first waves of European explorers and settlers in the early modern period brought social change to the Americas, Asia, Africa, and other regions: both the new economic demands and the influx of administrators, traders, and foreign settlers into colonized societies altered the course of people's everyday lives there. These changes accelerated in the 19th century. Colonial bureaucracies composed of both local people and colonizers grew. Increasingly, foreign bureaucrats brought their wives and families with them, making new intrusions on the colonized. Having medical personnel on hand became crucial to maintaining the health of colonial armies, while missionaries felt it even more urgent to Christianize newly occupied regions. Settlements for these foreign residents sprang up, usually modeled after those of the home country, deliberately insulated as much as possible from native life. Once regions became the focus of multiple economic interests, investors joined traders in the work of developing wealth in the new market areas. Expanding economic opportunity often encouraged large-scale migration: after the mid–19th century, underemployed Spanish and Italian farmers headed for newly opened regions in French North Africa to set up farms and small businesses. Likewise, in the early 20th century Japanese farmers rushed to Korea to claim land. In these instances the native people were often driven from their farms violently or forced to work for the newcomers.

The new colonizers announced upon arrival that the regions they had conquered lacked governments, economies, and social institutions. This was not true: instead, the colonized peoples in fact faced an increased number of rulers and competitors for resources, because the newcomers added a layer of government to the already existing local and regional princes, chiefs of ethnic groups, heads of clans, and other local officials. Yet the native bureaucracies that the colonizing

British missionaries in New Guinea hoped to convert the natives to Christianity. Wherever they were based, missionaries aimed to instill in colonized people their own sense of proper religious practices, clothing, and knowledge

Missionary Imperialism

European and American missionaries travelled the globe in order to Christianize "heathen" peoples. Many also actively worked for the political takeover of African, Asian, and Pacific regions. In Bechuanaland John Mackenzie, a British missionary, found the Tswana eager for trade and technology but utterly resistant to Christianity. Its doctrines and set of social practices would upset their social and political customs. "The old feudal power of the native chiefs is opposed to Christianity," Mackenzie complained. When some of his converts contested the chiefs' traditional power, civil war broke out in 1878, with much of the anger directed against the missionaries. Mackenzie headed for London and with the help of the missionary lobby convinced the government that in the name of Christianity, civilized order, and economic development (gold had been discovered in the region) Bechuanaland should be made a British protectorate. In 1884 Mackenzie became the resident Commissioner there.

John Chilembwe, an African convert, baptizes his countrymen. In colonized areas many people adopted the religion of their conquerors, so that both Eastern and Western religions spread with the progress of imperialism.

powers mobilized to help them rule also offered opportunity for further education and upward mobility. For instance, the British took the lead in developing an Indian civil service. Foreign powers also recruited men in colonized regions into colonial armies, a practice many empire builders saw as enhancing their own might against the other great powers. The education of the natives was seen as important to teaching imperial laws and economic ways; consequently, new intelligentsias took shape that could deal in several cultural and political traditions. Mastering the colonizer's law, medicine, science, technology, languages, and social sciences put one in a different social niche.

Empire in the 19th and 20th centuries brought intense sexual contact, mostly between men from the imperial powers and women, girls, and boys among the colonized peoples. These contacts could on occasion produce long-term relationships, and the men involved often had multiple families. It is estimated that in the middle of the 19th century some 90 percent of British men abroad in the empire had a mistress from the colonized country. These sexual encounters involved prostitution, rape, and sex with children to satisfy the physical desires of the imperialists and their workers. The large cities to which displaced rural people flocked had tens of thousands of prostitutes in hundreds of brothels, specialized as to male or female houses. Because imperialism involved migration from a variety of countries, brothels with concentrations of French, Russian, and other national prostitutes arose too.

In some areas such as China and Japan younger daughters were regularly sold to brothel owners as small children to pay family debts or bring in needed income. In other regions like Africa historians judge that prostitution became a well-regarded way for women to boost their earnings and gain social status.

Whether they were the colonized or the colonizer, individuals took on new identities. Colonized peoples added new roles: personal servant to whites, concubines, day laborers, tax dodgers, consumers. But people from the imperial powers also played new roles as members of a superior race, big-game hunters, colonial soldiers, travelers, tourists, transnational migrants, or mothers of the next generation of world leaders. To fill these roles, citizens of the imperial powers learned to be healthier, to exercise and study more, and to understand and consume colonial products. By the end of the 19th century more men of the imperial countries had had military training as their armies grew larger, partly to meet worldwide imperial competition. In short, the coming of an international economy remade many of the world's societies.

Remaking the Ruling Class

The British attributed the vastness of their empire—in comparison to the lesser holdings of the French, Dutch, Germans, and Japanese—to the team sports that were becoming part of the curriculum in the exclusive, all-male schools and universities of Britain. Teaching sports likewise became a way of training, disciplining, and "improving" the men in the colonized populations who would become civil servants. Sports were seen as the standard of fairness to which everyone adhered. As team sports like soccer became popularized and professionalized late in the 19th century, working-class people developed team loyalties that were easily connected with national loyalties based on winning in sports.

Imperialized society thus brought about the change that the leisured aristocrat received far less respect than the vigorous and physically active man. In these excerpts from the writings of the Reverend J. E. C. Welldon, a former school headmaster in England, he discusses the various virtues to be gained from team sports and how these new attributes benefited the development of British global power.

Englishmen are not superior to Frenchmen or Germans in brains or industry or the science and apparatus of war; but they are superior in the health and temper which games impart. . . . I do not think I am wrong in saying that the sport, the pluck, the resolution, and the strength which have within the last few weeks animated the little garrison at Chitral . . . are effectively acquired in the cricket-fields and football fields of the great public schools [private schools in England], and in the games of which they are the habitual scenes. The pluck, the energy, the perseverance, the good temper, the self-control, the discipline, the co-operation, the esprit de corps, which merit success in cricket or football, are the very qualities which win the day in peace or war. The men who possessed these qualities, not sedate and faultless citizens, but men

Liberation Cricket

The English game of cricket was originally a popular sport played in rural villages and towns. In the 19th century the Victorian middle and upper classes took the game over in the sense that they made it emblematic of the values that were said to produce British supremacy. They maintained that the game represented fair play, uprightness, and self-discipline.

Cricket, like other aspects of British culture, migrated to the empire, where natives could admire it. In the West Indies cricket took hold of the popular imagination: "Black people are particularly enthusiastic about the game," one observer noted. "It is quite common to see tiny black children innocent of clothing indulging in it with all the assurance of their elders, using, however, sugar canes for wickets, coconut palm leaf for a bat and whatever they can lay their hands on for a ball."

Soon, however, the West Indians became better at the sport than their masters. In 1900 they were admitted to the all-white team for international competition: "Without these black men it would have been quite absurd to attempt to play first-class counties [in England]," an official claimed. By the 1920s blacks were the big stars of the teams, gaining social mobility. However, they also made cricket their own by introducing well-defined West Indian moves and stances in batting, in a "calypso" style, as some called it. Batsmen like Learie Constantine became international celebrities.

of will, spirit, and chivalry, are the men who conquered at Plassey [site of British victory in India, 1757] and Quebec. In the history of the British Empire it is written that England has owed her sovereignty to her sports. . . .

It is my earnest desire that athletic games should be kept pure of all that may lower the spirit of the game. For the lesson of fair play in sport is the lesson of honesty in business; and, as I have traveled over the world, I have been scarcely less struck than pleased by finding that foreigners, though they do not always give English merchants credit as the equals of Germans, or even of Japanese, in industry or ingenuity, or in the persistency of advertising their goods, yet acknowledge the good faith of British merchants as delivering goods which, whether they are entirely up-to-date or not, are always trustworthy alike in their material and in their manufacture. . . .

One remarkable instance of fighting at Harrow [School], if only one, I still recall. Among my pupils there was an Egyptian boy of high rank, who was admitted to the school, I think, at the instance of Lord Cromer [heard from earlier on the subject of Orientalism], as it was judged on political grounds to be important that his education should take place in England rather than in France. One morning this boy appeared in school with two black eyes. I wrote to his house-master, asking him, if possible, to find out who had been fighting the Egyptian boy. After some inquiry, he sent me as the culprit, the last boy whom I should have suspected of an aggressive pugilism. I said to him, "B—, you have been fighting. Have you any excuse to give?" He hesitated a moment, then he raised his eyes and said apologetically, "Please sir, sir, he said something bad about the British race." The only possible reply which I could make was: "That is enough, my boy; you may go."

"He had broken one of the first rules of the game, which is that a black boy must never shoot without orders, unless his master is down and at the mercy of a beast."

—U.S. safari organizer Carl Akeley on slapping his "gun boy," Gikungu

Another change brought on by the development of imperial societies was massive killing of large animals like elephants, lions, and tigers in organized expeditions through Asia and Africa. Before the middle of the 19th century such expeditions by whites had been comparatively rare, with hunting remaining mainly an activity of indigenous men who needed the food and other animal products. Imperialists came to dominate hunting, as they did politics, by converting formerly independent hunters into their servants on these expeditions. Typically, local hunters demanded large amounts of meat from the kill as their payment. Such payments, plus the fortunes that were to be made in such treasured substances as ivory and the bloodthirstiness of many European hunters devastated the wild animal population.

As society imperialized and industrialized, conservation movements took shape late in the century, but the conservationists clamped down less on the amateur hunters than on the natives. In the German East Africa licensing program started for hunters, a native professional hunter of elephants for their ivory was charged 40 times what an amateur European was charged. These prices and the subsequent depletion of animals contributed to forcing colonized peoples to work for whites as auxiliary hunters as well as day laborers on plantations, in mines, and in other colonial labor.

The practice of hunting big game also came to make fine distinctions among upper-class European men, marking venturesome imperialists as superior to the stay-at-homes. One British hunter, an official of the East India Company in the 1830s and 1840s, here explains the difference.

Some imperialist women took advantage of the opportunity to break the female stereotypes in place at home, as Lady Curzon did on a big-game hunt in Asia.

Why the Gentlemen of England don't know what sport is. The knocking over a brace or two of partridges, and a hare or two in a little bit of a plantation, or an unromantic grain field, called by them *sport,* is not to be compared with Indian shooting. The one is confined in extent, the other boundless; the one dull and tame, the other exciting to a degree.

An occasional woman liked to show her colors hunting too as imperialism and the popularity of sport came to attract middle-class women. Kate Martelli, the wife of a British official and an avid hunter in India in the 1880s, wrote *Tigers I Have Shot* to document her kills to a disbelieving public.

As we waited, all sorts of creatures, scared by the beaters [local people assigned to drive out the game], passed us—pig and deer, pea-fowl and jungle fowl, the majestic sambhur [a large deer] and the pretty nilghai [a type of antelope], not to mention foxes and jackals, went by within shot, but for today, at any rate, they were safe. At last came the tiger. He advanced like an enormous cat, now crouching upon the ground, now crawling forward, now turning round to try and discover the meaning of the unwanted noise behind him. When he was about eighty yards from us, I fired and hit him on the shoulder; then the other fired and the tiger bolted. [Martelli, as the first to hit the tiger, was credited with the kill.]

Martelli's ability to discern many different species was part of hunting, and superior knowledge was part of being a member of a grand imperial race. Somewhat later, former President Theodore Roosevelt characterized a hunting trip to Africa as being part of a scientific expedition to study wildlife and fauna when it was in fact a rampage of animal killing. As a deputy of the governor of Kenya recalled, Roosevelt was "utterly reckless in the expenditure of ammunition, and . . . he so unduly exceeded reasonable limits, in certain species. . . ." Wanton killing, it was said, made it easier to slaughter resisting natives and built up a matter-of-fact attitude toward the murder of local people that kept imperialism going, as one British soldier put it.

For the amount of big game I shot during my first tour in Kenya I have no excuse. I am not proud of it, neither am I ashamed of it. When I arrived in the country I was obsessed by an unashamed blood-lust. Hunting is man's primitive instinct, and I indulged it and enjoyed it to the full. In Kenya's early days fresh meat was not easy to obtain. The African was loathe to part with his stock and there was no European settler in the country who could provide meat. Also, when travelling with from 20 to 200 healthy Africans, all doing hard work, meat becomes almost essential, and more than three-quarters of the animals I shot went to provide meat for hungry and deserving mouths.

Sir Frederick Lugard, an administrator who began his career by making a fortune killing elephants for ivory, thus explains hunting as a way of exerting power in colonial society.

I used the meat proportionately; those who had marched most willingly, carrying the heaviest loads, and giving no trouble, received the largest share, while some, who had been laggards and grumblers, got none. Such a division, of course, takes much time; but I found that there is no more effective way of maintaining a good spirit in the caravan, and of saving the necessity [of] flogging and such like punishments. The common custom, I believe, is for the meat to be thrown, as it were, to the dogs—either scrambled for or left to the head man to divide with what favouritism or carelessness they like. . . .

An illustration from The Lake Regions of Central Africa *by the adventurer Richard Burton reveals the importance of the local worker or slave and the commercial importance of the trade in ivory. Travel memoirs often contained illustrations of such striking scenes along the author's itinerary.*

Women participated in exploration, missionary work, and many other aspects of imperial conquest. By the end of the 19th century some of them found traveling through the empire to be intellectually stimulating and socially liberating from the conventions that governed European middle-class women's lives. A passionate collector of butterflies, or lepidopterist, Margaret Fountaine was one of those who traveled outside Europe as much as possible to find adventure and pursue her interests. The many findings of "new women" armed with cameras and other advanced technology contributed to the holdings of anthropological and natural history museums, foreign journalism, and collections of exotic specimens that made the great powers indeed imperial societies.

At the same time, imperialism was changing the definition of what women could be and do. An English clergyman's daughter born in 1862, Fountaine kept a secret diary that surprised its readers, when it was finally opened in 1978, for its accounts of her love affairs. While her butterfly collections were famous, the extent to which such "new women" were likewise pioneers in redefining social roles has not been fully understood. Here is a tale that begins the story of Fountaine's long relationship with her Syrian guide, Khalil Neimy, in 1900–1901.

I went back to Athens for two nights, but longed to be back in the wild, free to lead my own unsophisticated life, away from the conventionalities of civilization. Freedom is the crowning joy of life. Thank God there are few on earth I really care for; I would there were none. I want to see all I can of this beautiful world before I have to leave it, and life is so distressingly short. It is the affections that hold us back from great enterprises, it is the affections that tie us down to one spot on earth—if not in body, in spirit. And then at the end of it all life is over and we have accomplished none of those great things our soaring imaginations once led us to suppose were to be achieved. . . .

At Ain Sofar . . . not a man offered to help me—the Syrians and the Turks are

Lord Curzon and his American wife ride an elephant on a tiger hunt. Although the British believed their own identity to be superior, they simultaneously tried to be like the Indians.

not a gallant nation. However, I ordered one to help me with [my trunk], and being told to do so he lent a hand readily enough. I found a man and mule waiting for me, and we had not gone more than a quarter of an hour when I saw some butterflies new to me— no other than the Syrian *Doritis Apollinus* which I had never seen alive before. . . .

The drive to Baalbek took about four hours. When we were alone and no one else could see us under the hood, Neimy kissed me repeatedly on my hands and arms, and as I felt in a thoroughly "loose" mood that day, I raised no particular objection to his doing so. . . .

Those first days at Baalbek were fraught with blind entreaties and mad infatuation, till I began to think that I had made a mistake in engaging Neimy as my courier for the summer. I had longed sometimes to have once more a lover, but after this, never again. It was only the day after our arrival that he suddenly threw his arms round me and tried to kiss me on my face by force. I was furious at his assurance, and for fully half a minute I struggled to free myself from his grasp. . . . But alas for the weakness of human nature, only the very next day on the mountain side under the shadow of some huge rocks in one of the quarries in the neighbourhood of Baalbeck, I sank lower than I had ever sank before; the very audacity of the man overcame my sense of all that was right and proper. Why are men such animals?

Imperializing Local Elites

Imperial powers changed the positions of local rulers, bringing them into the new governing system of indirect rule. Imperialism has long been seen as a form of insurmountable global power. In fact, as a political system it was not unified and sometimes did not even work at all, resulting in situations in which the imperialists had simply to give up control, as occurred in parts of Africa. In order to have any chance at ruling these far-off realms, much of the time imperialists used local bureaucracies that were already in place, employed local chiefs, or designated as "chief" a local personage who caught their eye as being particularly useful. These local rulers entered the imperial system with both their new and old roles to play. In this official report the British governor of Nigeria explains the system of indirect rule through chiefs.

The English lepidopterist Margaret Fountaine expanded Western knowledge of butterflies. As imperialism opened up regions to travel for scientific discovery, women who had trouble getting academic or scientific jobs in their home countries found opportunities for study and adventure abroad.

Imperialism set off a new genre of travel novels for young Americans. like those advertised on the page of a 19th-century magazine. Along with such books, which were heavily advertised in popular magazines, tourist guides, art posters of exotic places, cameras, and special travel paraphernalia whetted the appetite for places that were sold to potential consumers as "exotic."

The policy of the Government was that these chiefs should govern their people, not as independent but as dependent Rulers. The orders of Government are not conveyed to the people through them, but emanate from them in accordance where necessary with instructions received through the Resident. While they themselves are controlled by Government in matters of policy and importance, their people are controlled in accordance with that policy by themselves. A Political Officer would consider it as irregular to issue direct orders to an individual native, or even to a village head, as a General commanding a division would to a private soldier, except through his commanding officers. The courts administer native law, and are presided over by native judges (417 in all). Their punishments do not conform to the [British] criminal code, but on the other hand, native law must not be in opposition to the Ordinances of Government, which are operative everywhere, and the courts . . . are under the close supervision of the District Staff. Their rules of evidence and their procedure are not based on British standards, but their sentences, if manifestly faulty, are subject to revision. Their prisoners are confined in their own native gaols [jails], which are under the supervision of the British staff. The taxes are raised in the name of the native ruler and by his agents, but he surrenders the fixed proportion to Government, and the expenditure of the portion assigned to the Native Administration, from which fixed salaries to all native officials are paid, is subject to the advice of the Resident, and the ultimate control of the Governor.

Local civil employees of the imperialist powers worked with at least two societies—that of the colonizer and that of the colonized. Because a member of the local bureaucracy learned the laws and customs of the imperial power, he also had a great deal of information about institutions back in the imperial homeland, such as parliaments, constitutions, universities, learned societies, and political clubs. Colonial officials encouraged local elites to value the way of life of the colonizers, even through imitation. Local activism developed in the form of scientific clubs, political action groups, and reform societies.

Sayyid Ahmad Khan, an employee of the British civil service in the Indian city of Aligarh, was a loyal Muslim and Indian nationalist as well as a loyal functionary for the British. He founded a Science Society as well as the Aligarh British Indian Association because of his belief in working through fair British institutions. Here is how he explained the society at its inaugural meeting in 1866.

In order to get our rights from the Government the Indians must establish contacts with the [British] Parliament. During the East India Company's rule, India's great difficulty was this: all of its affairs had access to the Company's Court of Directors only and were scarcely settled by the Parliament. Now the Indian administration has been taken over by the Queen and Indian affairs will have connection with the Parliament. In order to adequately inform the members of the Parliament of our affairs and reasonable aspirations we should create channels of communication.

An East African official, formerly a sultan (a Muslim ruler), was part of a layer of local leaders impressed into service by the imperial powers to lessen the cost of ruling distant colonies. Instead of ruling according to local customs, such officials followed the rules and customs desired by the imperial power—in this case, Germany. The result was often the destruction of traditional ways of life.

Like those Englishmen who reside in India and have decided to create an association in England, similarly we should establish an association for all the Districts of the North West in order to communicate our aspirations and objectives to the Government and the Parliament.

Sayyid Ahmad Khan, as a loyal Muslim, might have been expected to receive guidance from and direct his allegiance to the Caliphate, the institution succeeding the prophet Muhammad to rule the Muslim community. Khan disputed this expectation, however, showing that he defined himself as a subject of a mighty Western power. He thus exemplified the power of imperialism to transform identity.

We cannot possibly be considered subjects of the Turkish Caliph. His Sovereignty does not extend over us. We are residents of India and subjects of the British Government, which has guaranteed us religious freedom. Our life and property is protected and our personal affairs—marriage, divorce, inheritance, endowments and wills—are administered according to the *Shari'a* [Islamic law]. In such matters even Christian judges are forced to apply the Islamic laws to Muslim litigants.

Criticism from those colonized greeted these transformations of local identities during the course of imperialism. They were seen as antipatriotic, uncivilized, irreligious, and even laughable. In 1882, Mokshodyani Mukhopadhyay, an author, founder of a women's journal, and member of an influential political and literary family in Bengal, wrote the following controversial poem criticizing middle- and upperclass Indian men who seemed to adopt Western ways. She did so in response to a widely circulated poem insulting Indian women as vain and superficial. However, in this counterattack by her, Westernization is the chief flaw in men even as Westernized men are the chief flaw in Indian society. Only this excerpt of her poem "The Bengali Babu" exists today, found in an anthology of Indian women's writings.

Who's that rushing through his breakfast and bath?
The Bengali babu! He's terribly pressed:
The sahib will scold him, should he be late
So he's got to get ready, and bustles about.

There he comes, decked in trousers and jacket!
On his head a pith helmet, tied round with a scarf.

Alas, there goes our Bengali babu!
He slaves away from ten till four,
Carrying his servitude like a pedlar's wares.
A lawyer or magistrate, or perhaps a schoolmaster,
A subjudge, clerk, or overseer:
The bigger the job, the greater his pride;
The babu thinks he's walking on air.
Red in the face from the day's hard labor,
He downs pegs of whiskey to relax when he's home.
He's transported with pride at the thought of his rank—
But faced with a sahib, he trembles in fear!
Then he's obsequious, he mouths English phrases,
His own tongue disgusts him, he heaps it with curses.
The babu's learned English, he swells with conceit
And goes off in haste to deliver a speech.
He flounders while speaking, and stumbles and stutters,
But he's speaking in *English*; you must come and hear.

Alas, there goes the Bengali babu!
Cane in hand, wearing shoes, smoking a cheroot;
Some, sahib-fashion, are hatted and coated.
Not a thought of religion, they lie about and sing.

He longs to be fair, scrubs vigorously with soap;
Rubs a towel till his skin peels off;
Parts his hair in front in the style of Prince Albert,
Scents himself liberally, and reeks like a civet.

Social Reforms

Colonized elites started working to change their own societies according to the models of the imperial powers. For instance, in Europe the idea that the upper classes could remake the working classes into better people like themselves had led to the development of settlement houses and other institutions for social reform. Influenced by these ideas of reform and charity, well-to-do local elites in the colonies set up their own societies in the 19th century to help orphans, the homeless, unwed mothers, and other

unfortunate people. In India the caste system, in which people were born into unchangeable and hierarchical social groups, relegated some to "untouchable" status. Untouchables did the most menial work, and the better people avoided them because they were said to bring physical and spiritual contamination.

Contact with empire brought different ideas about caste and led to reforms, some of them amounting to an attack on the social structure. An upper-class Indian woman here recounts in a letter to her spiritual advisor an argument with her family about her philanthropic work.

Letter to Jotiba Phule, 10 October 1856

While we were talking one day, Bhau said, "You and your husband have rightly been excommunicated. You help the lowly castes like the mangs and mahars and that, undoubtedly, is committing sin. You have dragged our family name in the mud. Therefore, I want to tell you that you must behave according to the customs of our caste and follow the dictates of the brahmins [the elite caste]." Mother became livid when she heard these wild and irresponsible remarks. Bhau is otherwise kindhearted, but he is extremely narrow-minded and he did not hesitate to criticize us and blame us squarely. Mother was distressed. She did not scold him but tried instead to reason with him. She said, "God has given you the ability to speak sweetly. It doesn't become you to misuse it so." To refute his argument, I said, "Bhau, your point of view is extremely narrow and, moreover, your reason has been weakened by the teachings of the brahmins. You fondle even animals like the cow and the goat. . . . But you consider the mangs and mahars, who are as human as you, untouchables. Can you give me any reason for this? When the brahmins are in their 'holy' clothes, they consider you also untouchable and they are afraid that your touch will defile them. They treat you just like a mahar then." When he heard this, he turned red in the face and asked me, "Why do you teach those mangs and mahars? I can't bear it when people criticize and curse you and create trouble for you for doing that." I told him what the English had been doing for the mangs and mahars and said, "The lack of learning is nothing but gross bestiality. It was the possession of knowledge that gave the brahmins their superior status. Learning has great value. One who masters it loses his lowly status and achieves the higher one. . . . My swami, Jotiba, confronts the dastardly brahmins, fights with them and teaches

Unbound Feet

I . . . heard a speech delivered by Miss Chang Ching-hsien telling us that footbinding is contrary to the principles of Heaven and man and harmful to our country and people. One by one she eloquently attacked the evils of footbinding. It was such a good speech that since that day I have not bound my feet very tightly. One reason is that the pain is so hard to live with; another is that, although I wasn't able to unbind them then, I hoped to be able to do so someday. . . .

On Thursday I went with Sister Ch'a and met Jo-nan and Ya-nan and talked with them for a couple of hours. I was very impressed by them. They were most vocal and articulate against footbinding. . . . Chinese women have never considered themselves responsible citizens, and this has made China weak. . . . I have decided to unbind my own feet because I would be ashamed to go to meet anyone with these ugly bound feet. I discussed this matter with Eighth Sister, and we decided to unbind our feet now and in the fall to enroll in the Literary Society School.

Your sister, Shu-hsien
fifth day, fourth month, 1903

Footbinding, in which a girl's feet were broken and tightly wrapped, produced feet that were smaller than a teacup. While Chinese women poets often celebrated these tiny feet and the graceful women who tottered along on them, Chinese reformers came to see footbinding as a sign of backwardness. That was the imperialist view, too.

the mahars and mangs because he believes that they are human beings and must be able to live as such. So they must learn. That is why I also teach them. What is so improper about it? The brahmins believe that this will create problems for them and therefore they chant the mantra 'Abrahmanyam' ['Unholy!'] and go on reviling us and poisoning the minds of people like you.

"You surely remember that the English government had organized a ceremony to felicitate my husband in honor of his great work and had put these vile people to shame. Let me assure you that my husband does not merely chant God's name and do pilgrimages like you. He is doing God's own work. And I help him in that." Mother and Bhau were listening to me intently. Bhau repented what he had said and begged me to forgive him. . . .

With most humble regards,
Yours,
Savithri

Some Chinese writers advocated ending the practice of footbinding as early as the 18th century. This custom arose centuries ago for reasons that remain unclear. It involved the painful folding under of half of each foot in young girls and bandaging it to make the foot small, as tiny as three inches. Christian missionaries also encouraged reforming this practice as part of ending China's supposed "barbarism" and having it become civilized in a Western manner. The interference of these missionaries in a custom passed down from mother to daughter is a topic of debate today. Was their interference, people ask, not merely an imposition of Western ideas, no matter how much reform might have reduced women's suffering?

A strong movement against footbinding developed late in the 19th century, but it entailed creating ways for reform-minded families whose daughters did not bind their feet to find husbands. In a society where marriages were arranged by parents instead of by the young people themselves, what family would want to accept a bride so "deformed" as to have regularly sized feet? Thus not only did reform involve changing a deeply entrenched, traditional practice, but it meant setting up new social arrangements for finding marriage partners. Here are the bylaws of the Anti-Footbinding Society in Hunan, China. Although this society looks traditional because it continued the custom of arranged marriages, the society believed itself to be promoting "modernity."

1. The purpose of organizing this society is to provide opportunities for members to arrange marriages for their children so that girls who do not bind their feet will not become social outcasts. For this reason, society members must register the names and ages of all their children, and this information will be made available to all members in their selection of mates for their children.

2. Every member is entitled to make selections among the registered children. However, marriages with nonmembers' families are allowed if the young ladies do not have bound feet.

3. In selecting mates for their children, members must observe strict compatibility of age and generation. Furthermore, no match can be made unless both families agree to it. No member is allowed to coerce, intimidate, or use any other forms of undesirable persuasion in arranging a marriage. . . .

5. A matchmaker may be engaged to arrange the marriage contact. Local customs and rituals may be followed regarding the exchange of gifts. The society suggests that frugality and simplicity be observed by all members, regardless of how wealthy they are. . . .

7. The marriage ceremony should be discarded because ancient rituals are no longer suitable for today. However, members are allowed to follow the commonly accepted rituals and ceremonies of the Ch'ing dynasty because sometimes, for the sake of expediency, we have to do what others do. However, the society recommends that members be guided by frugality and simplicity.

8. The clothing worn by members' daughters should conform with the accepted style. However, their footwear should conform to the style of their brothers. There should be no exceptions, because other styles of footwear may be shocking and offensive to other society members, thus injuring the girl's chances for marriage.

9. If people want to have worthy daughters, then they must promote women's education. If men want their wives to be worthy, then they must donate money to establish local women's schools. . . . By helping other people's daughters learn, one also helps one's own wife because only after women's education has been popularized can the foundations of a marriage be solid.

Like these Chinese heading for the railroad station, people under imperial rule used the conveniences introduced by their masters, becoming travelers and tourists themselves. Attitudes changed in some cases, as some of these travelers attended universities, came to practice medicine and other professions, or took up the cause of liberating their countries from imperialist rule.

New Identities

As empires developed, single men emigrated to join colonial armies and bureaucracies, to work in mines, or to find employment in cities. Colonial officials sponsored brothels for members of the armed forces and recognized that the growth of cities based on the labor of single men uprooted from their families in rural areas would encourage prostitution. From the 1890s on, Nairobi, Kenya, was one of these rapidly growing cities where colonial officials worked to organize and regulate prostitution. But in the first decades of the 20th century the practice was carried out in private houses, often insulated from official view. While ordinary prostitutes, who themselves came in from the country to find opportunity, made the most money from white colonizers, their regular customers were usually African laborers. Male migrant workers living under imperialism needed and paid for a variety of domestic services, which allowed for prostitution to blend with ordinary life and for colonialism to function more smoothly than it might have otherwise. One Nairobi prostitute explained the system in this way.

They knew that the house belonged to a woman who never had a husband, so they knew it was a safe place to come because the owner had no husband to beat them. If a man saw me and liked me, then he would come to my door and knock and ask to come in. . . . The best way to find men was for them to come to your room and talk, you make tea for him, and you keep your house clean, you keep your bed clear, you have sex with him, and then he gives you money. . . . I didn't go openly looking for men, and men came to my room with respect, no one could tell that they were boyfriends and not my husband just from looking. . . .

If you spoke to these men, and told them about yourself, and kept your house clean, and gave them bathwater after sex, he would give you a few more pennies, and if he liked you he would come again, and if he came again, even to greet you, you would give him tea, and if he came again for sex you would also give him tea, and then he would have to give you even 75 cents. . . . If a man knew you and came to you regularly, he could give you as much as a shilling, but if he was a stranger to you it would be 25 cents.

Meanwhile, prostitutes themselves formed new networks and families to replace the rural families they had left far

behind. **They were especially drawn to Muslim society for its nurturance and for its support of women's ownership of property. As a result of prostitution, many women in Nairobi owned property. This prostitute talks about her new city "mother"—another example of an identity created by imperial modernity.**

She was a Kikuyu [an African ethnic group], but she was a Muslim . . . called Mama Asha. . . . She's my first mother because she's the one who helped me when I came to Nairobi, she's the one who gave me my first place to live, she taught me to speak Swahili, and she's the one who gave me the new name of a Muslim woman. She made me become a Muslim, that's why I call her my mother and her own born sons my brothers. . . . You know, in those days no man would love you if you already had a baby. Most of the girls, they waited until the baby was born and then would kill the baby or abandon it to die. . . . In those days you couldn't tell your real mother that you were pregnant, your real mother could never allow you to have a baby when you weren't married, she must not know. . . . Many prostitutes here in Nairobi had old woman mothers who cared for them and gave them names like Mama Asha did for me. . . . That's the kind of woman who can teach you the right way to behave in town. They would say "now you are my daughter, don't kill the baby, you must take care of the baby." That's how I learned that the mother I met here in town was better than the mother who gave birth to me, because she is the mother who can hear that you are pregnant and tell you truly the right thing to do.

Imperialism brought with it a brisk trade in commodities of all kinds, including raw materials, huge capital goods such as locomotives, and small consumer goods. As colonized people became part of the cash economy, they came to have small amounts of money to spend, and established contact with the consumer market. New goods came to intrigue them as they did the colonizers. This porter who worked for the Germans in East Africa reported how he spent the seven rupees he was regularly paid.

I bought myself many things. I bought loincloths and shoulder cloths. I bought these cloths for three rupees. I also bought tobacco from the market and soap too. At the same time I bought manioc and groundnuts for the home journey. But none of us thought of buying sugar. Because when we saw sugar, we said: That is salt. None of us had ever seen white sugar.

Japanese tea house girls sometimes also served as courtesans. Prostitution swelled with the growth of cities in both imperial and colonized countries. In the West, newspapers attracted readers with stories of a global "white slave trade" in young women and girls. Such articles turned the tables on colonized peoples, making them appear to be the oppressors of the white race.

Chapter Five

Imperial Culture

From the beginning of the 20th century, Europeans and Americans alike began praising a unique "Western civilization"—a culture that, they claimed, made people in the West far different from those who were colonized. But a close-up look at imperialism shows that, in fact, under its influence cultures became intermingled: hybrids were created as different stocks were grafted together. Both the colonizers and the colonized were transformed, and never more so than in modern times, as rapid communications and transportation made the globe seem smaller. On the simplest level, most Europeans drank coffee and tea and ate sugar, chocolate, tomatoes, and a host of other new foods—all products originating on different continents; they wore pajamas and eventually sandals—just some of the clothing adapted from tropical regions. As mass marketing started to develop at the end of the 19th century, new techniques of poster advertising used the exoticism of colonized regions to sell goods, using print techniques for the posters that were themselves copied from the printmakers of Asia.

Although the Europeans and Japanese often thought they were bringing civilization to less developed peoples, instead the national cultures of the imperial powers were profoundly redefined by their contact with the colonized peoples' way of life and their skills. Intense debates over the merits of Western versus non-Western culture, over what languages one should speak and what was good art, became central to national life. Many of these debates took place in newspapers, with both the imperialists and the colonized building mass circulation through publicizing the news of imperialism.

Culture also changed with the application of ideas from the developing social sciences—especially anthropology and sociology—to issues of racial and ethnic difference. The practitioners who came to be known as social scientists explained the concept of race as being based on what were said to be scientifically demonstrated facts of infe-

Giuseppe Verdi's opera Aida *premiered in Cairo in 1871. The use of Egyptian settings on stage and Egyptian motifs in art and architecture were part of a strong surge of Egyptomania that erupted with the building of the Suez Canal in 1869 and the British invasion of Egypt in 1882.*

riority and superiority. In this way, the superiority of one's race no longer depended on one's being a Christian or a pagan, but on a series of observable characteristics found in one's biological make-up: white skin meant superiority, colored signaled inferiority. This new "science" of racism worked to the advantage of the imperial powers. After the rise of imperialism there were few people in the West who were unaware of their skin color and an entire list of other features that were attached to the whole concept of race. However, race was now not just a matter (as it had been earlier) of what language one spoke or the length of time one's racial ancestors were thought to have inhabited the earth. Race was coming to designate who was better, smarter, worthier, more advanced. Thus a so-called scientific racial hierarchy entered culture, shaping people's thinking in harmful new ways.

Many imperial powers believed it their duty to "civilize" inferior natives by bringing them new culture and ways of thinking. The French, for example, defined imperialism as a civilizing mission and set up a vast network of schools and other institutions in Africa and Asia to spread French culture. Missionaries ran many schools, where they taught not only the "superior" languages (French, German, and Japanese, for instance) and "superior" history but deportment (one's personal conduct), domestic skills, and Christian ideas of morality. They worked to reform ideas about the family and women's roles, trying to turn women who were traders and agriculturists into middle-class housewives. Politicians from the great powers who would not grant their own women such rights as the vote, admission to the professions, or ownership of their wages and property nonetheless said that the treatment of women as being inferior in colonized countries was reason enough to establish imperial rule there. They attacked as barbarous the customs by which women wore head scarves or veils or bound their feet to make them small. And pressure from imperial culture did influence many upper-class women in colonized regions to abandon these traditions.

Just as the colonized peoples adapted to some Western ways through the pressure of imperialism or because they found certain customs, such as expanded education, to be advantageous, so were imperialist peoples

In the 19th and early 20th centuries, Western powers regularly held expositions of colonial arts and cultural artifacts from around the globe, such as the Congolese objects exhibited in Brussels in 1897. Expositions taught attendees about other cultures while also arousing their desires for colonial products.

An Indonesian village was constructed at a Dutch women's exposition in the 1890s to demonstrate what life was like in that important Dutch colony. Inside the main exposition hall, the life of modern Westerners was displayed as sophisticated and advanced compared to the wild and primitive life in the village.

like the western Europeans transformed in turn. They patterned their tastes in art, philosophy, religion, music, clothing, household decoration, and many other aspects of culture after those of the people they had supposedly mastered. Great philosophers like Friedrich Nietzsche, great composers like Richard Wagner and Claude Debussy, and great artists like Vincent Van Gogh and Claude Monet immersed themselves in ways of thinking and of creating art from societies around the world. New fields of study like anthropology took shape to attempt to understand other cultures. Outings to botanical gardens, zoos, circuses, and museums—all of them displaying global artifacts—came to be important to the citizens of the imperial powers. From at least the 19th century on, the most distinctive feature of what is called Western civilization is the way it depended on the rest of the world for techniques, ideas, inspiration, natural resources, human labor, and almost any other aspect of culture one can name.

Why Others Were Not So Good As the Imperial Powers

Ethnic differences and the form they took in physical features fascinated ancient peoples. Their explanations went in many directions. The Roman poet Virgil accounted for different skin colors as the product of different baking times each segment of humanity originally experienced in the process of creation. Much later, during the French Revolution, many

Evolution and Imperialism

Charles Darwin, an amateur British scientist, revolutionized ideas about the origins of human life in his highly influential book *Origin of Species* (1859). In it he maintained that life had developed over the course of millions of years rather than originating in a single act of creation. Darwin's writings also proposed that species evolved from lower to higher forms as a process of "natural selection"—meaning anything from warlike struggle for survival to the selection of mates. Thus he reasoned some characteristics die out and more advanced characteristics such as higher intelligence come into being.

Imperialists took Darwin to mean that "might makes right." Many believed that if they could defeat the peoples of Asia or Africa it was a sign of their own higher evolution, which made their victory a good thing. Darwin, however, saw violence as a lower form of existence that would give way to higher characteristics such as moral behavior among civilized beings.

argued vigorously that equal rights applied to all humans, no matter what the color of their skin, because all people were born equal in the state of nature. By the mid–19th century, as science and imperialism advanced hand in hand, scientists decided that they were the ones with the best insights into these differences. Looking at skin color, they said that this was just a sign of many other differences, including skeletal structure and brain size. In his theory of evolution, Charles Darwin contributed to the way in which these differences were made to appear scientific and hierarchical: nonwhites and women, he maintained, were less evolved than white men. Another influential contributor to the development of scientific racism was the Count de Gobineau, a French aristocrat, who wrote *The Inequality of Human Races* (1853–55):

I have shown the unique place in the organic world occupied by the human species, the profound physical, as well as moral, differences separating it from all the other kinds of living creatures. Considering it by itself, I have been able to distinguish on physiological grounds alone, three great and clearly marked types, the black, the yellow, and the white. However uncertain the aims of physiology may be, however meagre its resources, however defective its methods, it can proceed thus far with absolute certainty.

The negroid variety is the lowest, and stands at the foot of the ladder. The animal character, that appears in the shape of the pelvis, is stamped on the negro from birth, and foreshadows his destiny. His intellect will always move within a very narrow circle. He is not however a mere brute, for behind his low receding brow, in the middle of his skull, we can see signs of a powerful energy, however crude its objects. If his mental faculties are dull or even non-existent, he often has an intensity of desire and so of will, which may be called terrible. Many of his senses, especially taste and smell, are developed to an extent unknown to the other two races.

The very strength of his sensations is the most striking proof of his inferiority. All food is good in his eyes, nothing disgusts or repels him. What he desires is to eat, to eat furiously, and to excess. . . . It is the same with odours; his inordinate desires are satisfied with all, however coarse or even horrible. To these qualities may be added an instability and capriciousness of feeling that cannot be tied down to any single object, and which, so far as he is concerned, do away with all distinctions of good and evil. We might even say that the violence with which he pursues the object that has aroused his senses and inflamed his desires is a guarantee of the desires being soon satisfied and the object forgotten. . . .

The yellow race is the exact opposite of this type. The skull points forward, not backward. The forehead is wide and bony, often high and projecting. The shape of the face is triangular, the nose and chin showing none of the coarse protuberances that mark the negro. There is further a general proneness to obesity, which, though not confined to the yellow type, is found there more frequently than in the others. The yellow man has little physical energy, and is inclined to apathy; he commits none of the strange excesses so common among negroes. His desires are feeble, his will-power rather obstinate than violent; his longing for material pleasures, though constant, is kept within bounds. A rare glutton by nature, he shows more discrimination in his choice of food. He tends to mediocrity in everything; he understands easily enough anything not too deep or sublime. He has a love of utility and a respect for order, and knows the value of a certain amount of freedom. He is practical, in the narrowest sense of the word. He does not dream or theorize; he invents little. . . .

We come now to the white peoples. These are gifted with reflective energy, or rather with an energetic intelligence. They have a feeling for utility, but in a sense far wider and higher, more courageous and ideal, than the yellow races; a perseverance that takes account of obstacles and ultimately finds a means of overcoming them; a greater physical power, an extraordinary instinct for order, not merely as a guarantee of peace and tranquility, but as an indispensable means of self-preservation. At the same time, they have a remarkable, and even extreme, love of liberty, and are openly hostile to the formalism under which the Chinese are glad to vegetate, as well as to the strict despotism which is the only way of governing the negro.

Such is the lesson of history. It shows us that all civilizations derive from the white race, that none can exist without its help, and that a society is great and brilliant only so far as it preserves the blood of the noble group that created it, provided that this group itself belongs to the most illustrious branch of our species.

When it came to debating culture, some Europeans used Western art as the measure of all that was good and non-Western art as the symbol of inferiority. In the 1873 document that follows, the influential English essayist and critic John Ruskin presents the Western art of his day as the highest

> *"In regard to moral qualities, some elimination of the worst dispositions is always in progress even in the most civilized nations. Malefactors are executed or imprisoned for long periods so that they cannot freely transmit their bad qualities. . . . Violent and quarrelsome men often come to a bloody end."*
>
> —Charles Darwin,
> *The Descent of Man and Selection in Relation to Sex,* 1871

The captain of the Beagle, *the ship on which Charles Darwin ultimately devised his theory of evolution, drew the local peoples he encountered. Studying the facial contours and features of ethnic groups to show whether they were "primitive" or "evolved" became a major undertaking of scholars in imperial countries.*

Built in the 13th and 14th centuries as a great fortress for the Moors of North Africa who ruled Spain at the time, the Alhambra in Granada became a tourist site where modern travelers could see the remnants of an exotic Islamic civilization that the Europeans had conquered.

Tourism

Tourism arose in the mid–19th century but had its roots in millennia of travel by people around the globe to find new resources or to see different sights. Early pilgrims were also forerunners of tourism in that they sometimes traveled in groups or took well-worn paths to visit shrines, holy sites, and saintly religious leaders. In 1841, Thomas Cook set up an English travel agency that took people first around Europe and eventually to the wilds of the United States. So skilled did Cook's tour agents become that they even took responsibility for the movement of troops to Africa. Tourism also implies national or regional organization of sights, transportation, and lodging in order to obtain revenue, a crucial aspect of tourism that also developed in the 19th century.

form, but he also sees a time when Western art, like the current non-Western art, was not so highly evolved. The use of ideas about evolution and development showed that Ruskin worked with Western ideas of progress and Darwinian ideas that only some species evolved while others were left behind. Ruskin made the arts operate with the sciences to intensify cultural racism.

Observe, pleasure first and truth afterwards (or not at all), as with the Arabians and Indians: or, truth first and pleasure afterwards, as with Angelico and all other great European painters. You will find that the art whose end is pleasure only is pre-eminently the gift of cruel and savage nations, cruel in temper, savage in habits and conception. You will find this kind of formal ornamentation in . . . that "detestable" ornament of the Alhambra. All ornamentation of that lower kind is pre-eminently the gift of cruel persons, of Indians, Saracens, Byzantians, and is the delight of the worst and cruelest nations, Moorish, Indian, Chinese, South Sea Islanders, and so on. I say it is their peculiar gift; not, observe, that they are only capable of doing this, while other nations are capable of doing more; but that they are capable of doing this in a way which civilized nations cannot equal. The fancy and delicacy of eye in interweaving lines and arranging colours . . . seems to be somehow an inheritance of ignorance and cruelty, belonging to men as spots to the tiger or hues to the snake. . . . Get yourselves to be gentle and civilized, having respect for human life and a desire for good, and somehow or other you will find that you will not be able to make such pretty shawls as before. You know that you cannot make them so pretty as those Sepoys do at this moment. You will find yourselves, as you make yourselves more kind and good, more clumsy in that sort of ornament. If you want a piece of beautiful painted glass at this moment, you do not find that any benevolent Christian can produce it; you have to go back to the thirteenth or fourteenth century to the days of those precious sovereigns when the Black Prince killed two thousand men, women, and children before breakfast because he got into a passion.

Kaiser Wilhelm II of Germany and Tsar Nicholas II of Russia were cousins who maintained an intimate correspondence in English until they became deadly enemies in World War I. They shared many cultural attitudes, including a powerful dislike for people of non-European stock and for Jews. Their racism was part of elite culture, helped fuel their imperial

drive, and bound them and other members of high society together, as these excerpts from the Kaiser's letters to his cousin show.

April 16, 1895

Dearest Nicky,

I thank you sincerely for the excellent way in which you initiated the combined action of Europe for the sake of its interests against Japan. It was high time that energetic steps were taken, and will make an excellent impression in Japan as elsewhere. It shows to evidence how necessary it is that we should hold together, and also that there is existent a base of common interests upon which *all* nations may work in *joint action.*

The joint action referred to was in fact so successful that Japan was compelled to give up acquisitions from its 1894–95 victory over China.

July 10, 1895

Europe had to be thankful to you that you so quickly had perceived the great future for Russia in the cultivation of Asia and in the Defense of the Cross and the old Christian European culture against the inroads of the Mongols and Buddhism, that it was natural that if Russia was engaged in this tremendous work you wished to have Europe quiet and your back free; and that it was natural and without doubt that this would be my task and that I would let nobody try to interfere with you and attack from behind in Europe during the time you were fulfilling the great mission which Heaven has shaped for you.

November 26, 1895

The situation in the Far East has given you the opportunity of discussing it with my uncle. I thank you for the way in which you kindly alluded to my cooperation with Russia and the coaling station question. The development of the Far East, especially its danger to Europe and our Christian Faith is a matter which has been greatly on my mind ever since we made our first move together in the Spring. At last my

An American tourist rides high on a camel, while his servant is relegated to an ass. By the end of the 19th century seeing other civilizations, especially those ruled by the imperial powers, became part of an upper-class education.

thoughts developed into a certain form and this I sketched on paper. I worked it out with an Artist—a first class draughtsman—and after it was finished had it engraved for public use. It shows the Powers of Europe . . . called together by the Arch-Angel Michael,—sent from Heaven,—to *unite* in resisting the inroad of Buddhism, heathenism and barbarism for the Defence of the Cross. Stress is especially laid on the united resistance of all European Powers, which is just as necessary also against our common internal foes, anarchism, republicanism, nihilism. . . .

Educating for Inferiority

Those who believed in the superiority of the imperial powers were generally those who set the curricula of schools in Asia, Africa, and the Caribbean. Many imperialists did not believe that ordinary colonized peoples should learn to read or write much, if at all. Yet imperialists needed large numbers of officials who were educated in the imperialists' own culture in order to translate laws and regulations, collect taxes, and enforce order. An appreciation of European and Japanese accomplishments would, it was believed, also make officials more respectful. As warfare became more sophisticated, members of armies had to have some measure of literacy too. Education in native culture—for example, teaching the history of Africa—formed a very small part, if one at all, in schools set up by the imperial powers. Thus, the existence of private schools run by colonized peoples alone were seen as dangerous, as this Japanese official makes clear about Korean-run schools that taught Korean culture and history.

Among the private schools, there are schools that teach songs and use other materials which encourage independence and incite rebellion against the Japanese empire. This is forbidden, and utmost care must be exercised to ensure that the prohibition of these [activities] is enforced. Koreans themselves should deeply reflect upon the consequences of fostering this kind of thought. For instance, the cry for independence will eventually lead Koreans to rebel against Japan. Will this promote the happiness of Koreans? Japan will just suppress such rebellion with force. This will not hurt Japan; only Koreans will suffer.

Another Japanese official set limits on what the education it sponsored in annexed Taiwan should include.

St. Mary's Girls' School, Rangoon, was typical of the schools founded by missionaries in the 19th century. Such schools undermined the role of local religions, which had traditionally controlled education, and favored instruction in languages of the imperial rulers to improve students' chances for upward mobility within local society.

Education, that is, education in a colony, is not purely for the purpose of advancing education. A colonial education system must correspond to social conditions and the people's cultural level. It is absolutely inadvisable to offer advanced courses. Teaching such courses has often done irreparable damage. Thus it is imperative that careful attention be devoted to deliberation concerning the establishment of such facilities. Virtually all colonial powers pursue a policy of promoting vocation education to provide students with practical skills. The people of Taiwan should be taught practical skills too so that they may earn a living and enjoy happiness.

Russia's expansion into Asia and the Middle East gave rise to still other proposals for the most effective way to rule so many ethnic groups with their own religions, political systems, and cultural traditions. Dealing with culture was seen as crucial to maintaining order and a better alternative to using brute force. Here is one administrator's report in 1862 on governing newly conquered Muslims—a report that shows how complex the question of culture was to imperial domination.

It seems to me that the principal fault that is sometimes encountered even among persons in the government lies in an unconscious hostility toward an alien people and an involuntary tendency to force it into submission to our own habits and customs. The effects of this attitude are so strong that, penetrating to the lower strata of officials, they are frequently reflected even in trivial details of ordinary relations, in daily life, offending equally the sensibilities of all classes, from the highest to the lowest, from the most wealthy to the poorest. It may well be asked whether such moral oppression can breed devotion and love for the government among the people.

On the basis of these observations, I have formed convictions and rules by which I have guided myself throughout the period of my office. I believe it is important to win the greatest possible devotion of the territory to the government, and to administer each nationality with affection and complete respect for its cherished customs and traditions. The administrator, in my view, may only prepare the ground and point the way to improvements, but he must permit each nationality to contribute its share to general national progress consistent with its own particular conditions. In this respect the education of native women is, of course, of prime importance. Because of her influence upon the family as

A Togo School Exam in a German Missionary School, 1909

GEOGRAPHY

The following questions had been set as a task:
  a) The large states of Europe and their capitals.
  b) What are the names of Germany's most important mountains?
  c) What are the names of the most important rivers in Germany and in what direction do they run? . . .

AN ESSAY

The subject was: "What good things have the Europeans brought us?" . . .

HISTORY

The task set was: The reign of emperor William I and the wars he waged. Name those men who had especially supported his government.

China had a tradition of women artists, writers, and intellectuals, but public education outside the home broke with tradition of family training and circulation of knowledge.

a repository of the national manners and customs, a woman has an equal effect on the habits of the child, the adult, and the aged, and therefore she alone can change for the better the domestic customs that are the primary basis for general improvement.

That is why, in a territory where a need is felt for a transformation of customs, attention should be given first of all to increasing the number of schools for women.

The problem of such a transformation is more difficult among Moslem peoples, since their civil organization rests on the foundation of Mohammedanism, and all their rules are therefore at odds with the civil principles of Christian government.

Eradication of the [Moslem] clergy's influence must therefore precede all other measures. Yet direct action on our part can only strengthen the people's fanaticism. Hence, it is necessary in this area to find also some means, derived and formed within their midst, which, gradually undermining the importance of the Mullahs, would in time destroy the authority of the Koran.

The message of the cultural superiority of the imperial powers took hold, and traditional popular culture came under attack. In India, women street performers amused urban crowds by singing and dramatizing mythical stories. These stories involved promiscuous love affairs among gods and goddesses or traditional heroes and heroines. Singers used them as allusions to their own or their audience's problems with husbands and family. In the first song the young widow Ambalika objects to her mother-in-law's request that she bear the child of her brother-in-law in order to continue the family name.

If it has to be done,
Why don't you do it, mother?
People say—
As a girl you used to row a boat in the river.
Seeing your beauty, tempted by your "lotus bud,"
The great Parashare stung you, and—
There was a hue and cry;
You've done it once,
You don't have anything to fear.
Now you can do as much as you want to,
No one will say anything.
If it has to be done,
Why don't you do it, mother?

Another song is the complaint of Radha, lover of the noble—but terribly unfaithful—god Krishna and a plea for some relief to her dilemma of how to deal with his departure.

He has now turned into the darling of
His new young sweetheart, and is
Floating in eternal happiness!
Well! Let him be happy.
There's no harm done.
But why did he have to leave me
On the horns of a dilemma?

To Indian officials and wealthy traders who valued the claims to moral superiority made by middle-class imperialists, popular songs came to appear lewd. Their message was sacrilegious, these performers vulgar. The musicians and dancers were increasingly called dangerous influences by those who wanted Indian women to appear less in public and become more virtuously domestic like the ideal English woman. Articles representing the views of these elites appeared in Indian newspapers from the 1860s on. These are from the Bengali weekly *Somaprakash.*

One complained: Look at the streets of Calcutta, how the vulgar lower orders right in front of thousands of bhadralok [educated or wealthy elite Indian men], trampling on the chests of the powerful police force, go around wherever they want to, singing extremely obscene songs and making obscene gestures!

Another commented: Who that has any pretensions to polite taste, will not be disgusted with the vulgar mode of dancing with which our play commences; and who that has any moral tendency will not censure the immorality of the pieces that are performed?

And another: It is not possible for an uneducated young woman to remain unexcited with listening to episodes like Raas [Krishna's dance with the milkmaids]

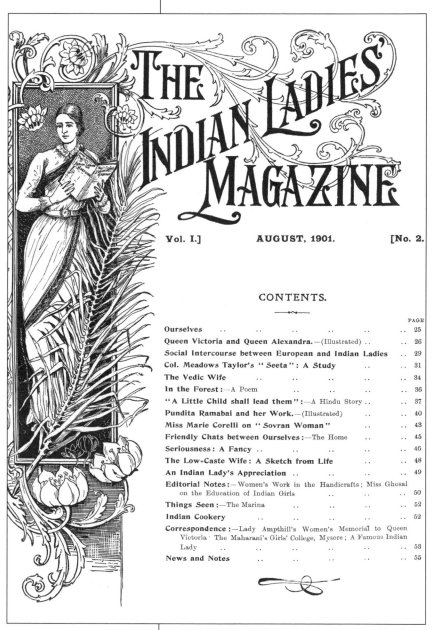

THE INDIAN LADIES' MAGAZINE

Vol. I.]   AUGUST, 1901.   [No. 2.

CONTENTS.

This magazine for upper-class Indian women intermingled articles on European travel with stories on the status of women in India.

"I skirmish in their [the natives'] streets, drive them pell-mell into the woods beyond, and level their ivory temples; with frantic haste I fire the huts, and end the scene by towing the canoes into mid-stream and setting them adrift."

—Henry Stanley, on his exploration of the Congo

or Krishna's escape with the clothes of the milkmaids. . . . Since it has become a source of so much evil, it is not advisable for bhadraloks to encourage it. Those who allow their ladies to go to kathakata [performances of mythical tales] performances should be careful. . . . If, during kathakata performances, women stay home and are provided with opportunities to listen to good instructions, discussions on good books and to train themselves in artistic occupations, their religious sense will improve and their souls will become pure and they will be suitable for domestic work.

Popular Culture Spreads Imperial Confidence

The superiority of the imperial races was epitomized in the great hero—the explorer or conqueror who triumphed over the forces of nature and the savagery of barbarous peoples. The hero celebrated himself in autobiographies and memoirs, and journalists built newspaper circulation by reporting on the hero's survival while scouting jungles, deserts, and mountaintops. The hero was feted in burlesque and vaudeville shows, and upon his death poets lauded him in somber, sacred tones.

The cult of the imperial hero was so powerful and enduring that it took later scholarship—some of it motivated by decolonization and civil rights movements—to see the hero as more savage, the colonized peoples as more active and sophisticated, and imperialism as less successful and complete than previously thought. Among those feted in his time, Henry Stanley was one of the most hard driving and brutal toward Africans. Pushing into the interior of Africa at any cost, including the slaughter of innocent people, he claimed the Congo region for King Leopold of Belgium. Here are two popular versions of Stanley's life, the first a worshipful ode written May 13, 1904, upon his death by the poet Sidney Low.

Large shall his name be writ, with that strong line,
Of heroes, martyrs, soldiers, saints, who gave
Their lives to chart the waste, and free the slave,
In the dim Continent where his beacons shine.

Rightly they call him Breaker of the Path,
Who was no cloistered spirit, remote and sage,
But a swift swordsman of our wrestling age,
Warm in his love, and sudden in his wrath.

How many a weary league beneath the Sun
The tireless foot had traced, that lies so still.
Now sinks the craftsman's hand, the sovereign will;
Now sleeps the unsleeping brain, the day's work done.

Muffle the drums and let the death-notes roll,
One of the mightier dead is with us here;
Honour the vanward's Chief, the Pioneer,
Do fitting reverence to a warrior soul.

But far away his monument shall be,
In the wide lands he opened to the light,
By the dark Forest of the tropic night,
And his great River winding to the Sea.

This popular song about Stanley in Africa was a hit in the 1890s in the London Gaity burlesque hall, a theater where ordinary people heard songs and watched comedians and other performers. It describes Stanley's last big expedition to Africa, which began in 1887 in order to rescue Emin Pasha, a high Egyptian official trapped by warfare. Stanley carried 100,000 rounds of ammunition on his rescue mission.

Oh, I went to find Emin Pasha, and started away for fun,
With a box of weeds and a bag of beads, some tracts, and a
    Maxim gun [an early machine gun].
I went to find Emin, I did, I looked for him far and wide;
I found him right, I found him tight, and a lot of
    folks beside,
Away through Darkest Africa, though it cost me lots of tin,
For without a doubt I'd find him out, when I went to
    find Emin!

Imperialism helped produce a new mass culture based on the widespread reading of newspapers. In the last third of the 19th century, with the spread of education for all children— not just the rich—and the resulting growth of literacy, news- papers became an important feature of every family's and

A pharmaceutical company marketed this stylish medical kit designed by Henry Morton Stanley. It contained necessities such as quinine that enabled Europeans to survive the many new illnesses they faced. Imperial adventure generated a host of such products.

every nation's life. They bound people of all conditions and all regions together through a common fund of information. Competition for this readership was intense; one way newspapers hooked readers was with lurid stories of sex, global adventure, and imperial war. Headlines screamed the latest on bloody imperial massacres or on the "white slave trade"—that is, the abduction of European women and girls for forced prostitution around the world.

Nowhere was the imperial theme developed with more journalistic intensity than in the United States in the 1890s, as wealthy tycoons and average people alike became ardently convinced that the prosperous, growing country needed an empire. The decaying Spanish empire in the Caribbean and Pacific caught the eye of rival newspaper owners Joseph Pulitzer and William Randolph Hearst, who used sensational or "yellow" journalism both to promote the outbreak of the Spanish-American War and to compete with rival papers. "Yellow journalism" was a tug-of-war for circulation built up by sensationalism in reporting, named for a popular cartoon called "The Yellow Kid" that appeared first in Pulitzer's paper, then in Hearst's. These excerpts from the dispatches of a foreign correspondent for the *New York World* in 1896 described the Cuban rebellion against Spain in such a way that war between the United States and Spain erupted in 1898. As a result of the U.S. victory, the country emerged as yet another strong player in the imperial struggle.

May 17, 1896

No man's life, no man's property is safe. American citizens are imprisoned or slain without cause. . . . The horrors of a barbarous struggle for the extermination of the native population are witnessed in all parts of the country. Blood on the roadsides, blood in the fields, blood on the doorsteps, blood, blood, blood! The old, the young, the weak, the crippled—all are butchered without mercy. There is scarcely a hamlet that has not witnessed the dreadful work. Is there no nation wise enough, brave enough to aid this blood-smitten land? Is there any barbarism known to the mind of man that will justify the intervention of a civilized power? A new Armenia [in 1894–96 the Ottoman Turks massacred tens of thousands of Armenians after they protested taxes and held demonstrations for religious freedom] lies within 80 miles of the American coast. Not a word from Washington! Not a sign from the president!

May 29, 1896

The skulls of all were split to pieces down to the eyes. Some of these were gouged out. All the bodies had been stabbed by sword bayonets and hacked by sabres until I could not count the cuts; they were indistinguishable. The bodies had almost lost semblance of human form. . . . The tongue of one had been cut out, split open at the base and placed on the mangled forehead in a ghastly likeness of a horn. Fingers and toes were missing. . . . Two of the mouths were split back to the angle of the jaw, so as to give an untellably ghostly grin to each mangled face. And the ears were missing. These could not be found and I was forced to the conviction of what I had often heard but never believed, that the Spanish soldiers habitually cut off the ears of the Cuban dead and retain them as trophies. Our Indians were more cleanly than this.

NAVAL OFFICERS THINK THE MAINE WAS DESTROYED BY A SPANISH MINE.

When war with Spain broke out in 1898 for control of Cuba, part of the American enthusiasm for war had been generated by blaring headlines reporting the explosion on the cruiser Maine off the Cuban coast. Reporters drew lurid scenes of blood and body parts and in total ignorance labeled the explosion the work of a bomb or torpedo. Behind the resulting war lay tens of millions of dollars in U.S. investments in the area and a strong desire to grab Spain's empire in Cuba, Puerto Rico, and the Philippines.

In 1889, France sponsored a Universal Exposition in Paris to commemorate the centennial of the French Revolution. This world's fair featured, among other exhibits from the colonies, Asian music and dancers, and was part of regular exhibits of world culture that took place from the mid–19th century on. The composer Claude Debussy was entranced by what he heard and saw at the 1889 exposition, returning many times to hear informal performances by the Indochinese and Indonesians. In particular he loved the gamelan, a group of performers on percussion and stringed instruments. Unlike Western music that worked according to a taut forward movement and in a linear fashion to resolve harmonic tension, this music was circular and more tranquil. Indonesian dancers did not perform classical Western ballet steps but were by turns languid, voluptuous, and majestic. Debussy's music soon changed; after that, Western music would never be the same.

The cultural influence from the colonies took several forms. In the first instance the rest of the world provided the subject matter for art, literature, and music: this had led to operas ranging from Wolfgang Amadeus Mozart's opera *Abduction from the Seraglio* in the 18th century to Puccini's *Madama Butterfly* in the late 19th. A second influence involved deeper themes behind stories: the composer Richard Wagner's many operas, including his four-opera cycle *The Ring of the Nibelungen,* underscored ideas of regeneration and renunciation taken from Buddhism and other Asian philosophies. Finally, Debussy changed the structure of his music, as would the composers who followed. In this journal article, he put forth the example of East Asian music to critique the West.

There used to be—indeed, despite the troubles that civilization has brought, there still are—some wonderful peoples who learn music as easily as one learns to breathe. Their school consists of the eternal rhythm of the sea, the wind in the leaves, and a thousand other tiny noises, which they listen to with great care, without ever having consulted any of those dubious treatises. Their traditions are preserved only in ancient songs, sometimes involving dance, to which each individual adds his own contribution century by century. Thus Javanese music obeys laws of counterpoint that make [medieval church composer] Palestrina seem like child's play. And if one listens to it without being prejudiced by one's European ears, one will find in it a percussive charm that forces one to admit that our own music is not much more than a barbarous kind of noise more fit for a traveling circus.

The Indochinese have a kind of embryonic opera, influenced by the Chinese, in which we can recognize the roots of the Ring. Only there are rather more gods and [there is] rather less scenery! A frenetic little clarinet is in charge of the emotionaleffects, a tam-tam invokes terror—and that is all there is to it. No special theater is required, and no hidden orchestra. All that is needed is an instinctive

The Indonesian gamelan is a cluster of gongs, xylophones, and other percussion instruments that provides music for puppet theater, dances, or plain listening. The gamelan accompanying Indonesian dancers at the Paris exhibition of 1889 was so powerful in its appeal to Claude Debussy and other composers that they went back day after day so that the music would sink in. In those days there were no recordings, only live performances.

desire for the artistic, a desire that is satisfied in the most ingenious ways and without the slightest hints of "bad taste." And to say that none of those concerned ever so much as dreamed of going to Munich [the Bavarian city whose king sponsored Wagner's experimental music] to find their formulae—what could they have been thinking of?

Much literature, such as Rudyard Kipling's stories and poetry, Olive Schreiner's *The Story of an African Farm,* or Joseph Conrad's *Heart of Darkness* directly described complex experiences of conquest and domination. But, as seen in the case of music, influences from the colonized could be subtler and actually more profound. Non-Western motifs infused literature and poetry as well as music to create the artistic movement called modernism. Modernism in the arts often relied on images rather than storytelling, or on fleeting impressions of characters in a novel, or in painting water lilies. But the use of these images as part of "modern" art also came from Asian aesthetic ideas. The avant-garde German poet Else Lasker-Schüler, who was considered a modern, "new woman," relied on the theme of an oriental rug and other exotic images to give spiritual force to her love poem "An Old Tibetan Rug." Asia, Africa, and the Middle East were seen at this time to have more depth in their spiritual philosophies and a more aesthetic or spiritual sense of objects, unlike the consumer values that Westerners had come to assign such things. Indian philosophy in particular proposed the merging of the individual into a great cosmic sea of being, while many of the Asian religions had a highly erotic side to them.

Both my soul and yours, which loveth mine,
In the Tibetan rug are intertwined.

Ray in ray, infatuated colors,
Stars that heaven-long wooed one another.

On this jewel our feet rest side by side
Thousand-upon-thousand-meshèd wide.

Sweet Lama son upon a musk-plant throne,
How long will your mouth likely kiss my own
And cheek on cheek the brightly knotted times go on.

Chapter Six: Picture Essay

Mixture

Cultural exchange has been a constant of human history for millennia, historians now know, because the migration of peoples took place even before recorded history began. But imperialism made those contacts intense and more graphic. The visual world of painting, architecture, furniture, fabrics, and many other artifacts changed because of imperialism.

Violence, travel, trade, technology, and changed ways of living were among the ingredients of imperialism. So were observing, borrowing, cultural mixing, and a new closeness—desired or not—of the world's people.

Did the imperial powers change more than those they conquered? Or is the reverse true? Colonized peoples had to adopt their conquerors' languages, clothing, and political ideas in order to survive. They learned the history, religion, and social customs of their colonizers in their schools. There was irreplaceable cultural loss—entire languages and systems of mathematics disappeared because those of Japan and the West were considered to have such higher value. By contrast, everything the West and Japan absorbed from colonized peoples was taken up voluntarily and enriched the cultural heritage and way of life of the conquerors.

It can also be argued, however, that colonization in particular transformed Western culture, which came to be an amalgamation of non-European food, music, art, architecture, patterns of thought, basic concepts, and games. Peoples in colonies or former colonies, the argument goes, value their own food, religions, belief systems, traditional clothing, and so on more than the imperial powers ever did. Resistance to the colonizers therefore took a cultural form. No one denies that imperialism involved intense cultural interaction, often with bizarre results. The late–20th-century Japanese composer Toru Takemitsu claimed that the major cultural influence in his life was the French composer Claude Debussy. Debussy, as discussed earlier, was most influenced by Asian music. Thus, in the case of imperialism it is often difficult to sort out what belongs to whom, and where one culture ends and another begins.

A wealthy American household is filled with products from East Asia, including a screen decorated with cherry blossoms, Asian statuary, and a lacquered writing desk. The recipient of the "New Necklace" (the painting's title) wears a silk smock, loose-fitting in a way that Western garments were not at the time and adorned with Asian motifs.

The building styles of European powers migrated to the countries they occupied. This private dwelling of the ruler of an Indian state has Western features such as porches, railings, and columns. Indian railroad stations in major cities were built in Gothic style or used the iron and glass construction standard in the West in the 19th century.

Sezincote, an English country home, was remodeled in the early 19th century to include an Indian dome. European buildings adopted a range of Asian and African architectural features. Kew Gardens, also in England, has a Chinese pagoda, and the entire style of domestic architecture called "Victorian" is adorned with curlicues and other wooden cutouts that appeared to be modeled after Chinese buildings. In Budapest, the museum of arts and crafts, built in the 1890s, combined designs from Hungarian folk motifs with Indian and Turkish features. Modern architecture features the clean lines of North African, African, Native American, Latin American, and Japanese dwellings.

Indian princes built or adorned palaces in mixed styles, including many rooms in which colors, lighting, proportions, placement of furniture, and even the furniture itself were distinctly Western—as in this Indian dining room. As with clothing, education, religion, and personal conduct, the decoration of houses indicated a mixed culture. Some scholars argue that this mixing was forced; others say it enriched the local way of life. Even liberation movements had mixed political aims, some of them—such as Marxism—borrowed from the West. It was only later that local culture gained value— particularly after Gandhi in the 20th century saw that desire for Western goods impoverished the country economically and culturally.

A Russian woman decorated her boudoir at Peterhof with Japanese wall coverings and upholstery. The Russian Empire looked toward many cultures. At the height of its power late in the 19th century rooms in royal palaces featured interior design from the Ottoman Empire and other regions. Catherine the Great had designed a "Turkish" room in the Hermitage in St. Petersburg and adorned it with many carpeted benches, intricate metal tables, and oriental rugs.

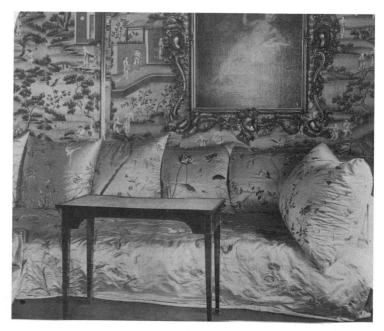

An ad for Pears' soap captures both the obsession with cleanliness and entrenched racism of Western imperialists. In an age when scientists were coming to understand germs and bacteria, cleanliness stood for superior understanding and scientific advance. Colonizers believed that one mark of their high level of civilization was the control of nature, including its insects, diseases, and dirt. Colonized peoples, by contrast, were considered disease-laden, filthy, and close to nature. The cleanliness that soap brought also stood for "whiteness," making the blackness of Africans automatically dirty. These values made soap and many other cleaning products cutting-edge consumer goods of the 19th century. Although the Africans stumbling upon this advertisement for the popular brand look puzzled and awestruck, it is an advertisement aimed not at consumers among colonized peoples but at Europeans themselves.

THE FORMULA OF BRITISH CONQUEST

PEARS' SOAP IS THE BEST

Since the late 19th century, advertising has spread ideas of fashions and other consumer items around the world. This Japanese woman has a decidedly Western look with her furs, uncovered shoulders, and conspicuous necklace. Her hair too looks Western, though her face is covered with cosmetics from Shiseido, a Japanese company. As Westerners adopted the looser and less confining garments of Asia and Africa, a composite global style emerged.

Cricket was taken up by Africans, Australians, New Zealanders, and West Indians in imitation of the English. But pursuit of the game was filled with controversy and racial strife, especially in the 1920s and 1930s as colonized peoples wanted greater recognition of their achievements. As teams from the colonies mastered the game, their excellence spread anger and even threatened the future of international competition. Yet some British people cheered the skill these newcomers brought to cricket.

The Indian game of pulah changed in the 19th century to become the British game of polo. The game involved horses and thus provided excellent training for horse and sportsman alike in the skilled riding necessary for imperial warfare. Pulah and polo both kept the soldier/player occupied during spells of peace in the often brutal contest for empire.

Despite traditional wisdom that East Asia refused foreign influence, this anonymous Chinese painting of the 18th century tells a different story. The composition, sense of perspective, colors, and poses of the main figures all borrow from the European tradition. The story would continue through the next two centuries. In the early 20th century, some Japanese artists rejected their native graphic tradition altogether, preferring paint and a compositional style that was first realist, then expressionist, and finally abstract.

Mary Cassatt's "The Letter" (1891) is Japanese in composition, color, perspective, and even in the figure of its main subject. Impressionists' "fleeting" sense of light and color reflected familiarity with the Japanese aesthetic idea of *mono no aware,* the breathtaking but ephemeral spirit of nature. The colors and compositional style of the great Western poster artists of the end of the 19th century also came from Japanese woodcuts, and bright posters were the major form of visual advertising at the time. Still another style, the collages developed by Pablo Picasso and other early 20th-century artists showed the influence of African masks often made up of bits of straw, string, paper, rocks, and other everyday items.

African emphasis on carving's utility as well as beauty yielded beautiful objects such as headrests, masks for ritual purposes, and useful bowls and dishes. African sculpture such as this head of an Englishman often served to warn people that the English were in the neighborhood at the moment. Historians suggest that some distorted or bizarre representations of Christian or European items are also signs of resistance to colonial ways.

The Italian artist Amedeo Modigliani, like many other artists of the early 20th century, helped shaped the idea of the "modern" in the arts by adopting African styles of sculpture. Pablo Picasso, Constantin Brancusi, and Barbara Hepworth are others who employed this borrowing to create a style that was seen by Westerners as fresh and original. Clean lines, lack of extra adornment, and figures that were exaggerated, not "realistic" or "literal," all helped define the modern arts. Were artists merely following an imperialist logic when they saw the conquest of these other cultural styles as part of Western progress?

P.J. LEMMER
65 JAAR

J.D.L. BOTHA
15 JAAR

S.J. PRETORIUS
53 JAAR

Chapter Seven

Rivalry and Resistance

Resistance to colonization occurred regularly as missionaries, traders, armies, and government officials brought chaos to colonial peoples' lives. Increasingly stubborn by the end of the 19th century, that resistance took many forms. One was the well-organized nationalist parties that developed, often led by those who had gained wealth under colonization or had received a Western education. Other resistance centered on reinvigorating traditional religious faiths such as Islam, because religion bolstered people's confidence, especially when confronting the heavy weapons of the colonizing armies. Religious revival was often connected to nationalist, ethnic, or other liberation movements. Although the African and Asian peoples put up continued armed resistance to the inroads of the great powers, colonization of necessity brought new forms of political action and consciousness raising.

The powers' rivalry for territory intensified simultaneously. Local clashes escalated into bloody wars that heated up the international scene. The British and the Boers, or Afrikaners (of Dutch or French Huguenot descent), fought each other in South Africa while the German Kaiser cheered Britain's enemies on. The French and British stood at the brink of war in Africa at the end of the 19th century, whereas Japan had its quarrels with any country—most notably Russia—that poached on its Asian ambitions. In 1894–95 Japan, showing the results of its rapid modernization, defeated China. Then anger mounted in Japan when the Western powers stopped it after this victory and reduced its gains. In 1904–05 the Japanese trounced the Russians in a stunning victory of East over West.

Colonized peoples the world over celebrated Japan's triumph, because it gave hope that European imperial powers could be defeated. (The fact that Japan also aimed to establish an empire was overlooked in the euphoria.) As the 20th century opened, armed uprisings multiplied. Yet hope that there was a way out of colonization soared

Boers were the descendants of Dutch and French settlers in South Africa, and they bitterly resented the British annexation of their territory in the 19th century. As British ambitions grew, the Boer War erupted between the two groups, making many in Europe believe that imperialism had gone too far.

The Boer War (1899–1902) was incredibly brutal and saw the first concentration camps. Many British back home were horrified at the herding of Boers—mostly women and children—into these camps and at the high mortality rate in them. Hostility to imperialism mounted as a result of this practice.

at precisely the moment when the imperial powers were developing even more destructive weaponry and naval might. The theories of U.S. naval officer and scholar Alfred Thayer Mahan that naval power was the key to empire led to an orgy of shipbuilding at the turn of the century. The rise of German, U.S., and Japanese industrial and military power made the established empires jittery that doom might lie just ahead. It was in this overheated climate of rivalry and resistance that early 20th–century imperialism unfolded.

Fighting Back

Political resistance can appear in all sorts of guises—in small acts of sabotage like work slowdowns or dramatic ones like assassinations. Stories of heroes provided models for action while songs, such as African-American spirituals, helped the oppressed endure so that they might someday take up the struggle more actively. Protestors drew on the history of their people's resistance to empire to shape their culture. In the Dutch colony of Curaçao, an island off Venezuela that served as a depot for the slave trade and also produced sugar, people rallied by singing of Tula, who had led a slave revolt in 1795, and by dancing the *tambú*. This dance was believed to be especially menacing because its performance was said to have led to the revolution. Even today, Curaçao's people need official permission to perform it. Curaçao remains part of the Netherlands, and this traditional song, "We're Headed for Porto Marie," remains in popular memory.

Concentration Camps

Although we associate concentration camps with the horrors of genocide in World War II, the first major system of concentration camps was started by the British in their campaign to defeat the Boers in South Africa. The idea behind these camps was to round up all Boer civilians in restricted areas or "concentration camps" so that the British army could efficiently sweep through the region and wipe out resistance. Although the motivation for these concentration camps was different from the motivation for the Nazi camps, the results were lethal for civilians. Disease spread through the camps, sanitary conditions were appalling, and people lived without any comforts. When the British reformer Emily Hobhouse arrived to report on the camps, her descriptions fueled outrage among many back home at the results of imperialism. Local African people were also forced into separate camps, where the mortality was equally grim. No reformer spread news of the Africans' situation, however.

(Chorus): We're headed for
Porto Marie.
Today we're going to
Porto Marie.
(Repeat.)
(Lead): A long time we've suffered
under the yoke of slavery,
but Tula has come and
wiped out all injustice.
(Repeat chorus twice.)
(Lead): We've long been in chains.
But Bastian has come
And broken all the chains.
(Repeat chorus twice.)
(Lead): Now we're going
my comrades
To Porto Marie.
Where we'll set out with all the soldiers.
(Repeat chorus twice.)
(Lead): There we will celebrate
our freedom.
Victory is on our side, comrades
Wecua is with us.
(Repeat chorus twice.)

The "Boxers" in China resisted the many inroads of Japan and the other imperial powers far differently. Imperial expansion in the 19th century had weakened the ability of the Qing dynasty to rule China. When in 1894–95 the Japanese defeated their vast realm in a short war, the government threatened to collapse. In addition to the great powers' control of many ports, bad harvests and droughts plagued the country in a situation that a group known as the Boxers attributed to the presence of Christians and foreigners. The Boxers were a secret society actually called the Righteous and Harmonious Fists—thus the nickname Boxers. The society's members claimed that the gods infused its members with heroic military powers. Discipline and the exercise of character in such rituals as boxing would allow the Chinese triumph over foreigners, end the drought, and revive the dynasty. Like many groups facing daunting imperial firepower, the Boxers' recourse involved drawing on such traditional sources of empowerment as religion and age-old rituals.

Many Chinese resistance groups stressed the equality of women and men. The Red Lanterns women's groups were as active as those of the men. The groups practiced their martial skills in public and gave theatrical shows and displays for city and village people. Taking the offensive, the Boxers and Red Lanterns ultimately fell to burning churches and the homes of foreigners and even slaughtering them. Only the colonial powers were strong enough to put down the Boxers. They used their victory over them in 1901 to exact even more from the Qing dynasty and to extend their control over China. Before their defeat, however, the Boxers' fame spread through popular poetry such as that below, which also encouraged resistance to foreigners.

Divinely aided Boxers,
United-in-Righteousness Corps
Arose because the Devils
Messed up the Empire of yore.
They proselytize their sect,
And believe in only one God,
The spirits and their own ancestors
Are not even given a nod.
Their men are all immoral;
Their women are truly vile.
For the Devils it's mother-son sex
That serves as the breeding style.
And if you don't believe me,
Then have a careful view:
You'll see the Devil's eyes
Are all a shining blue.
No rain comes from Heaven.
The earth is parched and dry.
And all because the churches
Have bottled up the sky.

The gods are very angry.
The spirits seek revenge.
En masse they come from Heaven
To teach the Way to men.
The Way is not a heresy;
It's not the White Lotus Sect.
The chants and spells we utter,
Follow mantras, true and correct.

U.S. marines were among those soldiers from the imperial powers used to put down the Boxer Rebellion. Rifles, revolvers, and artillery mowed down the rebels, despite their belief in the protective power of their spiritual rituals.

Raise up the yellow charm,
Bow to the incense glow.
Invite the gods and spirits
Down from the mountain grotto.
Spirits emerge from the grottos;
Gods come down from the hills,
Possessing the bodies of men,
Transmitting their boxing skills.
When their martial and magic techniques
Are all learned by each one of you,
Suppressing the Foreign Devils
Will not be a tough thing to do.
Rip up the railroad tracks!
Pull down the telegraph lines!
Quickly! Hurry up! Smash them—
The boats and the steamship combines.
The mighty nation of France
Quivers in abject fear,
While from England, America, Russia
And from Germany naught do we hear.
When at last all the Foreign Devils
Are expelled to the very last man,
The Great Qing, united, together,
Will bring peace to this our land.

Qiu Jin

Qiu Jin was a Chinese "new woman" at the end of the 19th century who had left her traditional marriage and two children to seek an education in Japan. Although she had wanted to go to the United States, it was Japan that opened her eyes to revolutionary ideas and movements. However, Qiu Jin was noteworthy in her own right: As one observer reported, "Was this person before me a man or a woman? A tall slender body bent slightly forward in Western male dress with a full head of trimmed black hair. . . . She carried a slender walking stick. Beneath her baggy trousers, worn-out shoes peeped through. A green necktie hung loosely over her chest." Qiu Jin claimed she had to dress like a man in order to gain male power. Back in China, she published a newspaper for women, worked as a teacher in a school for women, and worked for revolution. Qiu was captured by her government and executed in 1907. Full-scale revolution broke out in 1911 and overthrew the Qing dynasty.

Sometimes upgrading the status of women was seen as a key to liberation. In China, reformers identified women's weak position in the rigidly patriarchal traditional family with the general weakness of China. Because male privilege thrived by keeping women illiterate, inferior in their rights, and undeveloped in their knowledge of the world, the argument of reformers went, the entire nation was weakened. Although the Boxers worked to eliminate foreigners as a way of preserving China, other groups wanted to overthrow the corrupt Qing dynasty and enact Western reforms such as improvements in the status of women. They thus combined gender reform with national reform, as did movements in India and elsewhere.

In fact, by the turn of the century the Qing dynasty was coming to similar conclusions, even deciding to sponsor programs for elite Chinese women to receive an education in Japan as one way of improving China in general. However, the women who obtained this education, as in the case of the radical reformer Qiu Jin, wanted a complete overhaul of both nation and family—one that looked Western. One of many Asian and African women activists, around 1905 Qiu Jin presented the following manifesto for the liberation of Chinese women and the revitalization of China to meet the many threats to its future.

Oh, the most unfairly treated people in the world are we 200 million fellow women. Once born, it's better to have a good father; but if your father is a hot-tempered obstinate sort, when you open your mouth and shout "You good-for-nothing," it will seem as though he's sorry he can't grab and kill you. . . .

Grandmothers, you mustn't say that you're useless because you're old. If your husbands are really good men and they build schools for you, don't hinder them in any way. Middle-aged women, you mustn't oppose your husbands, diminish their fighting spirit, make them incapable of accomplishing deeds or seek your own fame. If you have children, please send them to school by all means. Girls, no matter what, never have your feet bound. Young women, if possible it's best for you to go to school; but even if you can't, then read at home and study your characters [Chinese letters] all the time. . . . Everyone, the nation is on the verge of collapse. Men can no longer protect it, so how can we depend on them? If we fail to rouse ourselves, it will be too late after the nation perishes.

If you seek to escape the shackles of men, you must be independent. If you seek independence, you must gain knowledge and organize. Women's education is becoming more popular in Japan, with each woman becoming expert in her own business and building a life for herself. They [Japanese women] are trying to rid themselves of a life without work of their own in which they are dependent upon their husbands. And, as a result, their nation is getting stronger.

The Great Powers Prepare to Take More

The European powers used Japan's defeat of China in 1894–95 to make new demands for access to the country and for monopoly control of trade—a process that came to be called "slicing the Chinese melon." The imperial powers also sent troops to crush the Boxer Rebellion, but instead of leaving after the rebellion was crushed, some refused to withdraw their troops. As these troops garrisoned various parts of China, it looked for a time as if China too would be carved up for good into national trade monopolies in which commerce with any particular region of China would be completely controlled by a single great power.

The United States, a growing industrial power, wanted its opportunities for trade to expand and not be closed off by the other imperialist powers. In 1900, U.S. Secretary of State John Hay announced the "open door policy," by which America advocated eliminating all barriers to free trade. This proclamation marked a new turn in imperialism, in which trade monopolies fell into disfavor among economic powers that did not already have empires. This kind of trade imperialism maintained the upper hand of the industrialized countries in their dealings with colonized or rural economies, whose trading positions remained weak. Here is one of Hay's Open Door announcements, made during the Boxer Rebellion itself.

We regard the condition at Pekin [Beijing] as one of virtual anarchy, whereby power and responsibility are practically devolved upon the local provincial authorities. So long as they are not in overt collusion with rebellion and use their power to protect foreign life and property we regard them as representing the Chinese

The beginning of the 20th century saw the United States joining those who claimed to be taking up "the white man's burden" of distant imperial rule.

people, with whom we seek to remain in peace and friendship. The purpose of the President is . . . to act concurrently with the other powers, first, in opening up communication with Pekin and rescuing the American officials, missionaries, and other Americans who are in danger; secondly, in affording all possible protection everywhere in China to American life and property; thirdly, in guarding and protecting all legitimate American interests; and fourthly, in aiding to prevent a spread of the disorders. . . . [T]he policy of the United States is to seek a solution which may bring about permanent safety and peace to China, preserve Chinese territorial and administrative entity, protect all rights guaranteed to friendly powers by treaty and international law, and safeguard for the world the principle of equal and impartial trade with all parts of the Chinese Empire.

The "open door" policy could change the way empire worked, making control more informal and behind the scenes. Or, given that much of the world was already divided up into empires, announcing such a policy could lead to greater competition among the powers and thus be destabilizing. The writings of American naval officer and historian Alfred Thayer Mahan became increasingly important in this climate because they suggested that success in trade and colonies depended on having navies and fueling stations where ships might be resupplied in the cause of trade mastery. Controlling the seas was more important, he argued, than occupying and governing vast stretches of land, though they often went hand in hand. Beginning in the 1890s, a massive arms race took shape among the great powers, with the construction of battleships as the top priority in military spending. Mahan's books, from which this analysis is taken, amounted to a blueprint that military men around the world followed as they mounted publicity campaigns for bigger, better, and more battleships.

The history of Sea Power is largely, though by no means solely, a narrative of contests between nations, of mutual rivalries, of violence frequently culminating in war. The profound influence of sea commerce upon the wealth and strength of countries was clearly seen long before the true principles which governed its growth and prosperity were detected.

Under modern conditions . . . home trade is but a part of the business of a country bordering on the sea. Foreign necessaries or luxuries must be brought to its ports, either in its own or in foreign ships, which will return, bearing in exchange the products of the country, whether they be the fruits of the earth or the works of men's hands; and it is the wish of every nation that this shipping business should be done by its own vessels. The ships that thus sail to and fro must have secure ports to which to return, and must, as far as possible, be followed by the protection of their country throughout the voyage.

This protection in time of war must be extended by armed shipping. The necessity of a navy, in the restricted sense of the word, springs, therefore, from the existence of a peaceful shipping, and disappears with it . . . a peaceful, gain-loving nation is not far-sighted, and far-sightedness is needed for adequate military preparation, especially in these days.

As a nation, with its unarmed and armed shipping, launches forth from its own shores, the need is soon felt of points upon which the ships can rely for peaceful trading, for refuge and supplies. . . . As there was immense gain, as well as much risk, in . . . early voyages, such establishments naturally multiplied and grew until they became colonies. . . .

The needs of commerce, however, were not all provided for when safety had been secured at the far end of the road. The voyages were long and dangerous, the seas often beset with enemies. . . . Thus arose the demand for stations along the road, like the Cape of Good Hope, St. Helena, and Mauritius, not primarily for trade, but for defence and war. . . .

. . . [T]he wise or unwise action of individual men has at certain periods had a great modifying influence upon the growth of sea power in the broad sense, which includes not only the military strength afloat, that rules the sea or any part of it by force of arms, but also the peaceful commerce and shipping from which alone a military fleet naturally and healthfully springs, and on which it securely rests.

From the Zambesi River in Mozambique, Africa, where this Portuguese gunboat was stationed, to the rivers of China patrolled by many of the great powers, many formerly independent regions had fallen under foreign rulership by the beginning of the 20th century. Foreign ships patrolling rivers, like foreign troops on one's soil, were a sign that whole regions had lost their sovereignty to the imperial powers.

Sigmund Freud

Sigmund Freud was a Viennese physician who held novel beliefs about the importance of dreams and about the existence of a realm of unconscious mental activity that had determining power over people's lives. These beliefs led to his theory of psychoanalysis as the cure for mental problems. Psychoanalysis involved talking about symptoms and signs, instead of confinement and other cruel treatment that mentally disturbed people usually received. Freud also discussed collective taboos, fetishes, and hysteria by looking back into early or "primitive" civilizations. Scholars have seen in his theories the influence of ethnographic writings on the trances, ritualistic healing practices, and other curative ideas of African, Middle Eastern, and Asian cultures.

Sigmund Freud, the influential founder of psychoanalysis, was, like many Europeans of his day, a collector of Egyptian and other so-called exotic or primitive statues. He also furnished the office where he practiced his new psychological therapy with Asian carpets and wall and furniture coverings.

Predicting the End

While some were plotting the expansion of trade and empire, others were glad to predict its overthrow. These predictions came from the heart of the great powers, first among the growing political force called socialism. By the end of the 19th century, socialist parties had become popular with millions of European men who had the vote. These parties were committed to ending capitalism, which they believed exploited workers in order to make profits for capitalists, and to ending nationalistic competition, which they were convinced kept workers blinded by patriotism and unable to see their own exploitation.

Instead of private property, socialism envisioned common ownership by workers of industries, large farms, and commercial institutions. Instead of nationalistic and imperialistic wars, socialists hoped for the brotherhood of man. For them, imperialism was "the highest stage of capitalism": when industrialists and bankers could no longer make enough profit at home, they argued, these capitalists had to exploit people through colonialism. One delegate introduced this resolution against imperialism at a German socialist party meeting in 1900; before World War I the German socialist party was the largest and most powerful of its kind in the world.

World or colonial policy, pursued for the sake of capitalist exploitation and the expansion of military power, as recently adopted with regard to China corresponds, above all, to the avaricious desire of the bourgeoisie for new opportunities to invest steadily increasing capital. They are no longer satisfied with the opportunities for exploitation at home. In addition, this policy expresses the desire for new markets that each country tries to usurp for its own. Such policies rest on the forcible appropriation of foreign territories and on ruthless subjugation and exploitation of their indigenous populations. . . . The Social Democratic [socialist] Party, the sworn enemy of oppression and exploitation of man by man, resolutely protests against this policy of robbery and conquest. The party demands that desirable and necessary cultural and business links with all the nations of the world should be established in such a manner that the rights, the freedom, and the independence of these peoples are respected and preserved.

A very different prediction of the end of imperialism came from some in the elite of the great powers. By the end of the 19th century an increasing number of Westerners had grown pessimistic about what the future held in store for them. For one thing, they saw themselves as in danger of being overcivilized and so prosperous as to tempt fate. For another, imperialism was becoming increasingly bloody, and it became evident to some that colonized people did not like their subservient condition and even hated Europeans for subjugating them. As the arms race escalated, imperialism threatened to pit the European powers against one another in some vast conflagration. The British poet and novelist Rudyard Kipling foresaw the end of the British Empire in his "Recessional," written in 1897.

God of our fathers, known of old,
Lord of our far-flung battle-line.
Beneath whose awful Hand we hold
Dominion over palm and pine—
Lord God of Hosts, be with us yet,
Lest we forget—lest we forget!
The tumult and the shouting dies;
The Captains and the Kings depart:
Still stands Thine ancient sacrifice,
An humble and a contrite heart.
Lord God of Hosts, be with us yet,
Lest we forget—lest we forget!
Far-called, our navies melt away;
On dune and headland sinks the fire:
Lo, all our pomp of yesterday
Is one with Nineveh and Tyre!
Judge of the Nations, spare us yet,
Lest we forget—lest we forget!
If, drunk with sight of power, we loose
Wild tongues that have not Thee in awe,
Such boastings as the Gentiles use,
Or lesser breeds without the Law—
Lord God of Hosts, be with us yet,
Lest we forget—lest we forget!
For heathen heart that puts her trust
In reeking tube and iron shard,
All valiant dust that builds on dust,
And guarding, calls not Thee to guard,

The passion for the trappings of naval power that now protected imperial might is seen in the fashion for sailor suits.

Personal adornment produced cultural mixture with a definite gender twist. For men, being modern and thus employable was illustrated by such a change of clothing. In their local clothing, women represented the force of tradition or local culture and habits. The evils of modernity were often equated in fiction with a Chinese or Indian or other Asian woman in Western clothing. Yet in the years after World War I, the nationalist leader of Turkey, Ataturk, decreed that men and women would all adopt Western clothing as part of his drive to make Turkey a modern power. Today, however, many national liberation, anti-Western, and fundamentalist religious movements advocate women—though not men—readopting the clothing of their pre-colonial society.

East Asian men as a group adopted Western dress more readily than women did.

For frantic boast and foolish word—
Thy mercy on Thy People, Lord!

Challenging the West

Although the Japanese had soundly defeated China in 1894–95, the great European powers stepped in to block their territorial gains. Russia used the opportunity, along with that offered in the Boxer Rebellion, to expand economically and militarily to Port Arthur, China, from which Japan had been excluded, and to other parts of the Far East. Meanwhile, the Japanese quietly increased their military spending. In 1904 they attacked Russia and—to the astonishment of the world—had won the war by 1905 in a series of bloody victories. As revolution erupted in its major cities, Russia reeled from this defeat. A former Russian finance minister, Sergei Witte, tried in his memoirs to explain the disaster as being the result of Tsar Nicholas II's personal weakness.

At heart, His Majesty was for an aggressive policy, but as usual his mind was a house divided against itself. . . .

He became involved in the Far Eastern adventure because of his youth, his natural animosity against Japan, where an attempt had been made on his life (he never speaks of that occurrence), and finally, because of a hidden craving for a victorious war. I am even inclined to believe that, had there been no clash with Japan, war would have flared up on the Indian frontier, or, most probably, in Turkey, with the Bosphorus as the apple of discord. From there it would have spread to other regions.

Almost contemporaneously, the Russian aristocrat Baron Nikolai Wrangel accounted for the defeat in different terms in his own memoirs.

What our son told us was not particularly reassuring. He said that the army in the field, both men and regimental officers were admirable, that the men were well-disciplined, would endure any hardships and were steady under fire, but they were short of many things, and the Staff were for the most part deplorable. Those who had capability were generally turned on to jobs for which they were unfit. For instance, General Mistshenko, an unrivalled artillery expert, had been placed in command of a cavalry corps of the advance guard, although he had never been on a horse, while

General Rennenkampf, a cavalry general if ever there was one, had been given the command of an infantry division. The state of affairs in the lines of communication was deplorable, and the worst of it was that revolutionary propagandists were at work, not only behind the lines but at the front. The Intelligentzia rivaled the Japanese agents in their zeal for spreading disaffection amongst the troops. My son could not say enough in praise of the Japanese army. They were admirable in every way; but all the same we must persevere. We should get them in the end. Only he wondered what would happen afterwards. Whether we won or were beaten we should have civil war.

In a speech in 1904 Count Shigenobu Okuma explained his country's military successes against Russia, stressing Japan's modernity and purposeful policies.

The recent development and prosperity of the Japanese Empire is no sudden and unexpected event which has come before the world without any adequate cause or reason for its coming into existence. It is the necessary outcome of certain causes well known to all who have studied our national history.

If we turn to the history of Europe we shall find one rule, to which there is absolutely no exception. Any nation, no matter what its constitution or form of Government may be, will prosper so long as it keeps itself swimming with the great current of human thought: to attempt to stem the current or swim against it, involves national ruin. There is no exception to this rule.

At the end of the Middle Ages, we find the people of Spain and Portugal full of a vigorous spirit of adventure: The discovery of America, the circumnavigation of the Cape of Good Hope, the opening of the new trade routes to India, were all due to their energy. . . . Spanish settlements were to be found in every quarter of the globe, and the name of Spain was feared and respected.

But her ruin soon came. The whole extent of her power scarcely covered two centuries of pleasant but profitless dreams. A few great nobles held the whole power; neither at home nor in their colonies were the people allowed the slightest voice or interest. . . . Russia is now following the bad examples of these countries. . . . An ignorant and arrogant hierarchy, an ostentatious Court, a corrupt moral atmosphere in the aristocracy, in the military and naval services, in the

"We [the people of the East] who are hated as cowards and imbeciles, are proud of this triumph of the East in its terrible struggle with the West. We heartily congratulate thee, Japan, on thy wonderful courage, thy discipline, thy iron will, and thy indomitable energy. . . . Thou alone hast saved the honour of the East, the downtrodden East."

—An Indian newspaper on the Japanese victory in the Russo-Japanese War, 1904–5

After Japan had defeated China in 1894, it imagined itself part of the imperialist "club." The European imperialists, however, firmly relegated Japanese to the category "inferiors" and saw in their victory a threatening "yellow peril."

The 1897 Sears, Roebuck catalog promoted corsets even as they were waning in popularity among American women. They restricted movement and often caused injuries to internal organs, and the curving figure that resulted came to indicate an old-fashioned attitude. As in the case of modern art, the streamlined figure of Asian and North African women was a sign of being a "new," progressive woman.

very entourage of the Czar himself, this is the poison that is destroying her life. Russia is trying to swim against the stream of human enlightenment. . . .

If now you will turn to the history of Japan, you will be able to see at a glance why it is that this Empire has always been so successful in all her undertakings. It is because our nation has always acted from the beginning on the principle . . . of "seeking knowledge throughout the world," i.e. of adopting what is good from every country, and entering into an honourable rivalry in culture and civilization with all nations throughout the world. . . .

The Japanese people is not merely a nation of fighters: it has no mean skill in agriculture, industry, and commerce, and if you will take the trouble to investigate the statistical tables of progress throughout the Empire, you will find that the national wealth has increased six or seven fold during the last thirty years. . . .

The origin of our modern Japanese development must not be sought in the opening of the country half a century ago. If you read her history for the last two thousand five hundred years you will find that her people have always possessed in a very high degree the power of assimilation. Japan came into contact first with the civilization of China, and assimilated it, without any trouble. When some years later the Buddhism of India invaded Japan through China, her native Shinto found a way to make room amicably for the newcomer, though in China a fierce feud arose between the followers of Buddha and those of Confucius. It is worth while noting that fifteen hundred years ago Japan understood and appreciated the principle of religious toleration. She was ready to welcome all that was good.

. . . [T]he present war is not one of race against race or religion against religion, but . . . the victory of Japan means the fusion into one harmonious whole of the civilizations of East and West.

Many colonized peoples in the upper classes organized to protect, if not liberate, themselves from the great powers. Inspired by the development of constitutional government that protected rights, they sought those rights for themselves within the imperial framework. Formed in 1885, the Congress Party of India was among the most prominent of these reformist organizations. A still different group took shape among Turkish military officers inspired by the Japanese victories to work for the revival of the Ottoman Empire.

The Ottoman Empire was widely seen as the sick man of Europe. Western bankers and industrialists had made inroads

on the empire through loans and industrial projects, while the British had virtual control of Egypt. In order to nibble away further at the declining empire, the great powers encouraged the different ethnic and religious groups under its sway in the Balkans to rebel against their Ottoman rulers. In response, the Ottoman sultan 'Abd al-Hamid tried to fortify the empire through modernization, educational reform, and arranging for a constitution. But at the first signs of trouble he closed down the new parliament, to the great distress of those who had benefited from his educational and other reforms. In 1908 a group of young officers forced the sultan to adhere to the constitution. At first Arab and then other groups in the Ottoman Empire applauded these efforts, but the Young Turks (as the reform-minded officers were called) quickly showed that they had no intention of advancing the rights of other groups in the empire. Their goal was to restore the empire to the ranks of true imperial power.

Together, the menacing reach of the great powers and the attempts to revive the Ottoman empire produced a pan-Arab movement composed of various like-minded societies. Pan-Arabism aimed to promote a sense of common identity among Arabs in the Middle East. This unity then encouraged opposition to both the Turks and the great imperial states through literary, theatrical, and political organizations. Instead of Western culture, the pan-Arab movement stressed the value of Arab ethnic heritage, and valuing this heritage built further resistance to inroads by foreigners. Here are the principles of one of these societies—tenets that attracted a growing following as the great powers developed their thirst for the region's oil resources.

1. The Arab nation is one great nation which has lost its magnificence and its independence because foreigners have gained control over it.

2. Because the Arab countries are rich countries, the Powers have ambitions, and strive to dominate them.

3. The Ottoman government, whose weakness and impotence were proven in the wars in Tripoli and the Balkans, will not be able to defend the Arab countries in time of need, should they be attacked by a powerful enemy.

4. The only way to change the situation is by strengthening the Arab element in the Ottoman Empire and turning it into one able to defend its own existence.

Women of the West Resist

The corset, designed to make the figure more slender, was an especially prominent garment in 18th- and 19th-century Europe. Men and women of the upper classes alike wore corsets in the earlier century, not only for enhancing the figure but for giving bodily support—though paradoxically the corset often weakened muscles and could lead to incapacitation. While men abandoned the corset in the 19th century as they donned comparatively shapeless suits, it became more widespread among women. It emphasized secondary sexual characteristics by lifting the breast and accentuating the hips. The constraints on movement offered by the corset have been compared to the constraints of footbinding. Both were painful garments, and reformers from the late 19th century on wanted to free up the female body.

Allowing for free movement, Liberty dresses were modeled after Asian garments and symbolized their wearer's modern, up-to-date attitudes. William Morris, his family, and his cadre of artisans were the initial designers of Liberty fabrics, which included motifs taken from Persian, Indian, and other Asian sources.

Chapter Eight

World War I

In 1914 war broke out among the great European powers: Germany and Austria-Hungary allied against Britain, France, and Russia. Turkey, Japan, Italy, and later the United States as well as smaller countries joined in, making the war global and involving the great powers' colonies. For decades, competition over colonies had provoked tensions, military skirmishes, and all-out war among the imperialist powers. An arms race and militant nationalism were directed against both the colonial subjects and the rivals for colonies. War rhetoric rang out in the European capitals.

The spark for war was the assassination of the successor to the throne of Austria-Hungary in June 1914, in Sarajevo, Bosnia, a region in the Balkans. The assassin, an 18-year-old Serb nationalist, hated great-power encroachments in the region. But this was only one of many seething movements for liberation flourishing in the Balkans, the Arab world, Africa, and Asia. For most of these nationalists the enemies were the imperial powers, including the Europeans, Japanese, Ottomans, and Americans. The rise of Japan and the subsequent revolt of the Turks against the Ottoman sultans discussed previously had inspired many of these rebels. However, as an ally of Russia, the Serbs were in a position to have their success in the Balkans affect the balance of power. Thus, Europeans went to war precipitously—to preserve this balance—but also confidently, because of their massive armies and huge buildup of weapons over the previous few decades.

As the war broke out, Britain and France were falling behind in a different kind of race—that for population. Because of the development of reliable contraception in the 19th century, birthrates in those two countries fell earlier than elsewhere, as the middle classes sought to improve their standard of living with smaller families. The new prosperity of Germany was boosting its population numbers because of improved health, but it was still on the edge of the birth-control revolution. Although everyone used colonial troops in World War I,

Colonial troops, such as this Ugandan color guard, served not only on the European front but in other contested areas such as Africa. British, French, and German troops carried on a less well-known struggle in World War I for control of colonies and their raw materials.

The scandalous Zimmerman telegram, once deciphered, showed a beleaguered Germany promising U.S. territory to Mexico if it would ally itself with Germany in World War I. Decoded in January 1917, the telegram, along with German submarine attacks, helped the U.S. decide to enter the war against Germany in the spring.

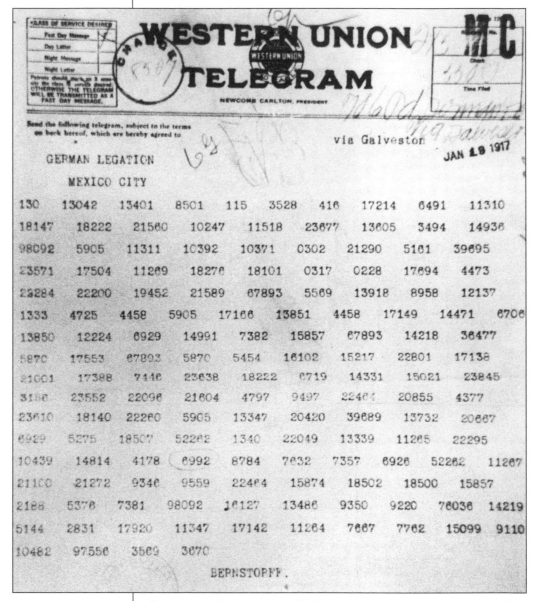

Britain and France controlled far more colonial peoples and thus had colonial troops that went toward making up their population deficit vis-à-vis Germany. A million Indians and hundreds of thousands of north and sub-Saharan Africans fought in World War I on the side of the British and French. Although in some parts of the colonies there was massive resistance to recruiting, the war met with expressions of loyalty from intellectuals, nationalist leaders, civil servants, and other members of the colonial middle classes. They expected that such loyalty would in turn bring respect, improved living conditions, and an extension of civil and political rights, even to the extent perhaps of self-government.

In general they were wrong. Colonial peoples died in massive numbers in World War I in every theater of the war. In Europe, they were usually placed in the very front ranks to head up the deadly advances against machine guns and other modern weaponry. Many colonial subjects were forced into wartime labor, and hundreds of thousands were shipped against their will to work in Europe. But when the war was over the victorious colonial powers—Britain, France, and Japan—included an extension of imperialism in the Covenant of the new League of Nations. They expanded their reach through the "mandate" system, under which the victorious powers took over the former German colonies as protectorates. Other regions that had hoped for independence after the war were also made into protectorates under the League of Nations' mandate system. Finally, the great powers brutally crushed movements in the colonies for improvements in their position, for liberation, and even for basic human rights.

The Race for Empire and the Race to War

Kaiser Wilhelm II longed for "a place in the sun" for Germany through turning to a successful "Weltpolitik" (global policy). Unlike Otto von Bismarck, the chancellor who had unified the German states in 1871, the kaiser wanted a striking global empire and would not be satisfied with anything less. A rapid buildup of the navy would serve these ends, the kaiser believed, so in 1899 he sent one of his best spokesmen, the state secretary in the foreign ministry, Bernhard von Bülow, to introduce his naval bill to the German Reichstag (parliament). Von Bülow did so with the warning—so much on Europeans' minds at the turn of the century—that nations came and went and disaster could be waiting just around the corner. Many historians believe that the kind of warlike rhetoric that came to infect the political debate of the times prepared the ground not only for imperialism but also for the vast war that broke out in 1914.

On one point there can be no doubt: world affairs are in a state of flux which no one could have predicted two years ago. [Commotion] Gentlemen, it has been said that in every century a struggle, a whole sale liquidation takes place which redistributes influence, power, and possessions across the globe: in the 16th

Richard Meinertzhagen was a soldier and spy who had served the British government in East Africa, the Near East, and in Europe. In 1917, before he was recalled to Europe to help in World War I, he disguised himself as an Arab in South Palestine. Imperialism and total war gave rise to spies and freebooters of all kinds.

MORE CULTURE

TO SAVE THE CIVILIZATION OF EUROPE

W. A. Rogers

As Germany enlists Ottoman support in World War I, this American cartoon of November 1914 mocks the idea that non-Westerners have any contribution to make to civilization.

century Spaniards and Portuguese divided the New World, in the 17th the Dutch, the French, and the English entered the competition—while we were busy bashing in our own heads [laughter]—in the 18th century the Dutch and the French lost most of what they had won to the English. In this 19th century of ours, England has expanded its colonial empire—the greatest empire which the world has seen since the Romans— farther and farther, the French have made inroads in North and East Africa and have created a new empire in Indochina, Russia is running its victory lap in Asia, which has taken it from the altitudes of the Pamir [Mountains, in central Asia] to the Pacific Ocean. The Sino-Japanese War four years ago, the Spanish-American war barely a year and a half ago have brought further changes, have brought about great, incisive, far-reaching decisions, have shaken old empires, have brought about new and serious ferment. No one can say what kind of consequences will come in the wake of the war which is presently engulfing South Africa in flames. [Hear! Hear!] The English prime minister said some time ago that the strong states will become stronger and that the weak ones will become weaker. Everything which has happened since proves the correctness of those words.

When the English speak of a Greater Britain, when the French speak of a nouvelle France, when the Russians open up Asia for themselves, then we too can claim a greater Germany. . . .

We must be secure from surprises not only on land but also at sea. We have to create a fleet strong enough to prevent the attack of any power. I emphasize the word "attack": because of our peacefulness, for us it is always only a question of defense. . . . I wish to stress that in reality things are not quite so simple and smooth as they might appear to someone with a lively and boundless imagination. It is not difficult to sit in one's study, atlas in hand and a cigar clenched between the teeth, contemplating new coaling stations, protectorates, and colonies. [Laughter] In real life, this is trickier: acquiring Kiauchow, the Carolines, the Marianas, Samoa for Germany was not quite so simple. . . .

Gentlemen, why is it that all other states are strengthening their fleets? Surely not because of the sheer pleasure of spreading money around. [Laughter on the left] Despite its financial difficulties, Italy is willing again and again to make sacrifices for its fleet. In France, the government can barely keep up with parliamentary requests for naval expenditures. Russia has doubled its naval construction. America and Japan are making a mighty effort, and England, which has the world's most powerful fleet, is continually adding to it. . . . I say that unless we build a fleet which is capable of protecting our commerce, our compatriots abroad, our missions, and the security of our coasts, we endanger the vital interests of our country. . . .

Imperialism prepared citizens to greet the outbreak of World War I with the kind of nationalist enthusiasm they had brought to watching sports or following the clash of armies in Asia and Africa. With some exceptions, men eagerly flocked to enlistment centers to join the war. In the colonies, officials and journalists usually greeted the war in terms that interpreted colonists' interests and those of the great powers as identical. As in Europe itself, opposition by socialists or national liberation movements seemed to give way to a real fervor for war. This comment on the outbreak of war appeared in the Bombay newspaper The Gujarti.

Hundreds of thousands of Indian troops served the British Empire during World War I. Because they were often put in the very front lines of any advance, their casualties were high and their experience of war extremely harsh. Nonetheless, until recently their participation in both world wars was invisible in history books.

Never in the history of British India has there been such an outburst of enthusiastic and fervent loyalty to His Majesty's Government as has been witnessed during the last few days since Germany and Great Britain declared war upon each other and Europe thus became involved in the gravest complications. The Indian people have held meetings throughout the country to give expression to their sentiments of profound loyalty and offer Government such help and assistance as lie in their power. Hindus, Majomedans [Mohammedans], and Parsis have already offered and have resolved to offer prayers to the Almighty for the success of the British arms, and the whole country has as it were been moved to its depths by an overpowering consciousness of the impending danger. The deputation from the National

Congress now in England have sent a letter to the English press, conveying to the King-Emperor an expression of their loyalty, emphasizing that whatever be the differences in times of peace, all Indians are united to Britain in times of war.

The colonial troops mustered by the European powers fought everywhere during World War I, but did so especially hard on the Western Front, which stretched from the North Sea coast through France to Switzerland. Warfare in the European theater was murderous, involving forced advances into lethal machine gun fire, months and years spent in foul trenches strewn with waste and parts of dead bodies, and, later, intense suffering from chemical warfare. Colonial troops were often sent to the very front of these lines of trenches, closest to the enemy and the line of fire. Here a white soldier describes the suffering of men from the tropics.

Our black troops were really pitiful. Collar pulled up, chechia [brimless, cylindrical caps] pulled down over their ears, the Senegalais shivered, huddled around the fires, and snuggled together in a clump like kids. Nothing worked. The troops from Martinique also froze, muffled up in their scarves. Before they were seen playing prisoner's base, at leap-frog, and other teenaged games, which made them look like exotic high-schoolers. But now they don't have the same taste for fighting the cold. Many black soldiers fall ill or go lame. Shouldn't we both wonder that more haven't fallen and admire the endurance of these poor men who suffer much more than whites. . . .

A corporal from Dahomey in western Africa gives a taste of life in the trenches.

In the course of this horrendous struggle I don't recognize myself anymore. Am I dead, am I alive? I can not say. . . . I have heard . . . the screams of the wounded, the hoarse groans of the dying, the pleading of my unfortunate comrades who crawl on the ground that is red with their blood. From this consecrated ground I picked up a human fist which I put immediately in my pocket as an eternal souvenir of peaceful and noble France. I have kept it religiously. It is my own relic, this thing. What miserable crowned head was able to order such horrors!

Broken Promises

Along with using coercion, colonial powers promised their colonized subjects that if they participated in the war a new era of cooperation, rights, and other benefits would open up to them. During the war the imperial powers also worked to upset the enemy's control of their colonial territories. In this official document the British and French alliance promises that it will grant independence to subjects of the Turkish empire, an ally of Germany, in return for their support.

The end which France and Great Britain have in view in their prosecution in the East of the war let loose by German ambition is the complete and definitive liberation of the peoples so long oppressed by the Turks and the establishment of national Governments and Administrations drawing their authority from the initiative and free choice of indigenous populations.

In order to give effect to these intentions France and Great Britain are agreed to encourage and assist the establishment of indigenous Governments and Administrations in Syria and Mesopotamia, which have already in fact been liberated by the Allies, and in countries whose liberation they are endeavouring to effect, and to recognize the latter as soon as they shall be effectively established. Far from wishing to impose any particular institution on these lands, they have no other care but to assure by their support and effective aid the normal working of the Governments and Administrations, which they shall have adopted of their free will. To ensure impartial and equal justice, to facilitate economic development by evoking and encouraging indigenous initiative, to foster the spread of education and to put an end to the divisions too long exploited by Turkish policy—such is the role which the two allied Governments assume in the liberated territories.

The victory of the Allies over Germany and Austria-Hungary in 1918 brought down those empires along with the Ottomans in the Middle East and the Romanovs in Russia. As a result, many colonial subjects were encouraged that they would receive freedom. Many attended the peace conference in Paris to lobby the delegates there. Although the Allies had promised widespread liberation and the extension of rights to Germany's and their own colonies at the end of

the war, they did not keep these promises. Instead, the Peace of Paris and the Covenant of the League of Nations dismembered the Ottoman and German empires and distributed much of their territory and colonies to the victorious powers in the form of mandates or protectorates. As the Covenant of the League of Nations, Article 22, indicates, the victors justified their continued control by arguing that people in these territories were not yet ready for freedom. The mandate system was further elaborated in other documents that talked about the levels of civilization attained by various peoples still under colonial domination. This system outraged people in the mandated territories as being just another manifestation of imperialism and its accompanying racism.

1. To those colonies and territories which as a consequence of the late war have ceased to be under the sovereignty of the States which formerly governed them and which are inhabited by peoples not yet able to stand by themselves under the strenuous conditions of the modern world, there should be applied the principle that the well-being and development of such peoples form a sacred trust of civilization. . . .

2. The best method of giving practical effect to this principle is that the tutelage of such peoples should be entrusted to advanced nations who by reason of their resources, their experience or their

Massive crowds flocked in front of Constantinople's Mosque of Faith upon Sheikh Ul Islam's 1915 proclamation of war against Britain, France, and Russia as part of an alliance with Germany and the other Central Powers. The turmoil of this total war would destroy four empires—including the Ottoman Empire. Turkey was born as a modern nation-state, and Britain and France claimed much of the Empire's former holdings in the Middle East as mandates.

geographical position can best undertake this responsibility and who are willing to accept it, and that this tutelage should be exercised by them as Mandatories on behalf of the League.

3. The character of the mandate must differ according to the stage of the development of the people, the geographical situation of the territory, its economic conditions and other similar circumstances.

4. Certain communities formerly belonging to the Turkish Empire have reached a stage of development where their existence as independent nations can be provisionally recognised subject to the rendering of administrative advice and assistance by a Mandatory until such time as they are able to stand alone. The wishes of these communities must be a principal consideration in the selection of the Mandatory.

5. Other peoples, especially those of Central Africa, are at such a stage that the Mandatory must be responsible for the administration of the territory under conditions which will guarantee freedom of conscience and religion, subject only to the maintenance of public order and morals, the prohibition of abuses such as the slave trade, the arms traffic and the liquor traffic, and the prevention of the establishment of fortifications or military and naval bases and of military training of the natives for other than police purposes and the defence of territory. . . .

6. There are territories, such as South-West Africa and certain of the South Pacific Islands, which owing to the sparseness of their population, or their small size, or their remoteness from the centres of civilisation, or their geographical contiguity to the territory of the Mandatory . . . can be best administered under the laws of the Mandatory as integral portions of its territory. . . .

Enver Pasha helped lead the Young Turk Revolution of 1908—a reform movement inspired by the Japanese victory over Russia in 1904–5. Enver Pasha, a general, promoted the alliance of his country with Germany in World War I. At the defeat of the Central Powers, however, he fled and was ultimately killed in the civil war that broke out with the Russian Revolution.

Sensing Change

Blaise Diagne, a Senegalese who had served as a customs official in many parts of the French Empire and as chief commissioner of military recruiting in West Africa, was elected as a representative from the colonies to the French parliament in 1914. A constant advocate of colonial rights, he nonetheless supported unity with France and recognized that the war had made a difference not only among colonial veterans but also among white deputies. These excerpts from two of his speeches in 1924 show the variety of thought among peoples from colonized regions.

In effect this is the first time in parliamentary history that our metropolitan [French] colleagues have attended debates on the colonial budget in such numbers. We remember the lamentable fact that in the past, before the war, when a colonial got up to speak deputies would be bold enough to give newsmen a signal to protest and start an uproar.

We knew a time when a colonial representative rose to speak that from the deputies' section itself would come cries that only meant one thing: "When can we get rid of colonial representatives?"

The war has served as such a lesson that we can congratulate ourselves for the good fortune that each and every one of us in this assembly has the right, recognized by all, to represent the interests of our constituencies.

The presence of colonial deputies in the Chamber [is] the symbol of the spiritual continuity and the principles of France.

The presence of someone like me in the parliament is not the sign of more or less servility among electors: it indicates a national unity to which France has decided to give a practical reality in according to the colonies parliamentary representation.

Remembering the Colonial Dead

The imperial powers quickly erased the record of the massive, courageous participation of their colonial subjects in World War I, as they would do again in World War II. White veterans and the white war dead received unending tribute—cities, villages, and nations erected tens of thousands of monuments to their memory—but the colonial veterans were scorned. Many of these troops occupied Germany to ensure the keeping of the terms of the peace treaty; this provoked extreme outrage—"Die Schwarze schande" (shameful blacks) they were called.

In contrast, Léopold Sédar Senghor, the poet who became his country's first president when Senegal became independent in 1960, memorialized these colonial veterans in his poetry and was one of the few famous authors to do so.

To the Senegalese Sharpshooters Dead for France

Here is the Sun
That makes virgins' breasts bold
That makes old people on green benches smile

That would wake the dead under a maternal earth

I hear the noise of cannon—is it from Irun [a Spanish civil war battlefield then active]?

They're putting flowers on graves and warming up the Unknown Soldier.

You my dark brothers, no one names you.

They promise five hundred thousand of your children to the glory of the future dead, thanked in advance the future dark dead

Die Schwarze schande!

Listen to me Senegalese Sharpshooters, in the loneliness of black earth and death

In your eyeless earless loneliness, more than in my somber skin in the heart of the country

Without even the warmth of your comrades lying against you as once in the trench once in village palavers.

Listen to me, Sharpshooters with black skin, even though earless and eyeless in your triple enclosure of night.

We have not rented mourners, not even the tears of your former wives

—They remember only your great flashes of anger, preferring the ardor of the living.

The laments of mourners are too light

Too quickly dried the cheeks of your wives, like the Fouta waterfalls in dry season.

The warmest tears too clear and too quickly drunk in the corners of forgetful mouths.

We bring you, listen to us, we who would spell your names in the months when you were dying.

We, in these days of fear without memory, bring you the friendship of your peer companions.

Ah! that I might one day with a voice the color of glowing embers, that I might sing

The Friendship of comrades fervent as entrails and delicate, strong as tendons.

Listen to us, Dead stretched out in the water of the depths of the Northern and Eastern plains.

Receive this red soil, under the summer sun this soil red from the blood of white victims.

Receive the salute of your black comrades, Senegalese Sharpshooters

DEAD FOR THE REPUBLIC!

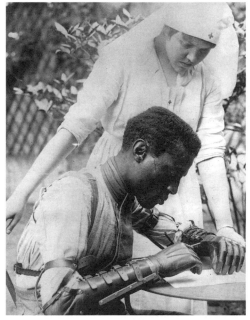

With the aid of a Red Cross nurse, a Senegalese veteran of World War I learns to write with his artificial hands. The heavy firepower of the war blew off limbs, destroyed faces, and ultimately produced a brisk industry in artificial arms and legs along with a growing plastic surgery practice.

Chapter Nine

The Torturous Path Toward Liberation

Rejecting violence, women followers of Gandhi march in protest against the British tax on a household necessity—salt. At the end of the war liberation movements welled up not only in India but around the world. The grievances of the colonial masses had become unbearable.

The broken promises of the war years would not go away, embittering colonial relationships still further. Even without these broken promises, World War I had changed things in a number of crucial ways. Some imperial powers—notably Germany and Russia—had collapsed as a result of the war, their monarchies toppled and new governments installed. In the case of Russia, the Soviet Union—the successor to the Romanov empire—had a socialist program that denounced imperialism. Yet the new government pulled its annexed territories (composed primarily of Muslims) into the socialist federation. Mired in war debt, the victorious powers had lost prestige, trade, and millions of men in the war. Colonial troops had seen the so-called civilized Europeans slaughtering one another by the millions with the utmost barbarism. And this shocking vision of the Europeans' weakness occurred simultaneously with growing prosperity outside Europe, even in the colonies. Europe had tossed away its prosperity and curtailed its trade to pursue a devastating and bankrupting war. Whereas Europe was suffering from devastation, falling birthrates, and loss of life, Asia was becoming increasingly urbanized, and its fertility rose.

Japan, on the victorious side in this war but far from its main battlegrounds, used the opportunity to make inroads into China and Siberia. It seized German possessions in the Pacific, which it then administered under the League of Nations mandate system. Its industries boomed during the war, to the point that Japan became a creditor nation. Then, ready to develop even more, Japanese businesses needed the markets, raw materials, and investments that could be found in colonial expansion. Simultaneously, the United States had prospered too, its businessmen like Henry Ford setting new trends in industrial production and management. Despite having a few colonies of its own, the United States wanted more than ever to enter the markets controlled by the other great powers. Targeted by these competitors and weakened by the war, the other Western powers also needed their colonies more than ever. The 1920s have thus been called the high tide of imperialism.

At the same time, riots—both spontaneous and backed by formal independence movements—erupted in the colonies. "Koreans everywhere are beginning to realize their common nationality," Maruyama Tsurukichi, the head of the Japanese police, announced after massive Korean riots in 1919. "It will be difficult to slow this trend or maybe even impossible to stop it." Reform organizations—from being small scale and composed mostly of middle-class intellectuals, businessmen, and officials among the colonized before the war—had become mass movements for liberation, capable of enlisting thousands of former soldiers. Calls for reform grew louder while colonial repression in many cases intensified.

Imperialism thus moved in contradictory directions and continued to be full of paradoxes. The 1917 communist revolution in Russia led to the formation of the Soviet Union in 1924. The policy of this new government included sending agents to secularize Muslim areas that had been annexed in the 19th century. Secularization meant, in part, teaching women to give up their traditional clothing and assert their rights to equality. In Western Europe and the United States, films, burlesque shows, popular songs, and fashion all continued to accentuate and appropriate colonial culture. In Paris, the African-American singer and dancer Josephine Baker performed to packed audiences as an exotic jungle creature, while *Tarzan of the Apes* (the story of a muscular native who learns Western ways and uses them in the jungle) and its sequels were best-sellers from the teens through the 1930s. Cultural mixture went both ways: as women in Egypt took off their veils and donned Western clothing, people around the world watched Western films featuring African or Asian settings.

As a result of the linked global economy, the economic depression that began with the crash of the U.S. stock market in 1929 encircled the world. Competition over markets and supplies of raw materials overheated and helped lead to World War II. One of the greatest paradoxes of these years was the role of Japan, whose dreams of conquering the Pacific world served to inspire anti-imperialists. Japan's imperial role in the staging of World War II ultimately made subject peoples' dreams of decolonization and freedom become a reality.

Escalation

Indian soldiers had served in great numbers in the European theater of war to defend the British Empire. And some 12 million Indians are said to have died in the global influenza pandemic of 1918–19 that resulted from the war. On their return home, many found not only that they were to receive no recognition in the form of new rights but that new decrees, such as one curtailing trial by jury, were actually moving counter to the promised improvements. Independence parties flourished, and mass demonstrations took place against the "Raj"—a Hindi word meaning kingdom or rule that had come to stand for British dominion in India.

Early in April 1919, local Indian leaders urged a work stoppage and a boycott of British products. Violence against the British erupted in Amritsar, one of the Punjab's major cities in northern India, where feelings against the new restrictions ran high. On April 13, the start of a major religious holiday, thousands of pilgrims from around the Punjab gathered to wait for observances to begin. Demonstrators joined the crowd in a large, walled-off square to plan their next move. Enraged by the boycotts as attacks against the British, Brigadier-General Reginald Dyer brought in troops and commanded them to fire on the estimated 25,000 to 30,000 pilgrims and protestors. Hundreds were killed in an event that has since been labeled "the end of the Raj." The blessings of civilization the British had claimed to bring had turned to massive, deliberate slaughter before the Indians' eyes. Here is how Dyer reported on the event to his superiors.

There was no reason to further parley with the mob; evidently they were there to defy the arm of the law. The responsibility was very great. If I fired I must fire with good effect, a small amount of firing would be a criminal act of folly. I had the choice of carrying out a very distasteful and horrible duty, or of neglecting to do my duty, of suppressing disorder or of becoming responsible for all future bloodshed. We cannot be brave unless we be possessed of a greater fear. I had considered the matter from every point of view. My duty and my military instincts told me to fire. My conscience

"Mussulmans and Hindus are united. I have been expecting this, there is a very big show coming."
—Brigadier-General Reginald Dyer, commander at Amritsar, to his son, 1919

The Salt of Freedom

The production of salt—a necessity in households around the world—was a monopoly of the British government in India. By this monopoly the British put a heavy tax on the natural salt it harvested and sold. It was illegal for any person living or strolling near the sea even to pick up salt. So, when Gandhi led a 240-mile march of his followers to the sea in 1930, it was no small matter. Picking up a lump of the salt, Gandhi publicized his civil disobedience, while his followers were arrested by the government. The nationalist and feminist poet of India Sarojini Naidu cried out at Gandhi's stunning deed: "Hail, law breaker."

was also clear on that point. What faced me was what on the morrow would be the Danda Fauj [Rebel Army]. I fired and continued to fire until the crowd dispersed and I consider this the least amount of firing which would produce the necessary moral and widespread effect it was my duty to produce, if I was to justify my action. If more troops had been at hand the casualties would have been greater in proportion. It was no longer a question of merely dispersing the crowd, but one of producing a sufficient moral effect, from a military point of view, not only on those who were present but more specially throughout the Punjab. There could be no question of undue severity.

The Amritsar Massacre might have triggered mass retaliation from the Indians, who were becoming increasingly politicized. But a new leader had taken charge of the anti-imperial movement, one who promoted a different kind of attack on British rule that emphasized a very pointed program of noncooperation and nonviolence. Although a variety of protestors called for temporary boycotts of British products and work stoppages, the lawyer Mohandas K. Gandhi built a mass movement by drawing many consumer and cultural issues into a political program. In this way his politics encompassed the full scope of imperialism. In the case of India, British imperial control was wide ranging, going beyond politics to make British clothing, language, sports, and other customs more attractive to the colonized elites than were their own. Gandhi built his movement around rejecting Western culture.

In economics, the British had taxed Indian raw materials such as salt and destroyed traditional Indian manufacturing of cloth and other products. Gandhi refocused his countrymen's attention on asserting Indians' rights to their own resources and traditions, but he did so by insisting that his followers not cooperate with British taxation, consumerism, and other practices that entailed their subjection. Noncooperation thus took its toll not only on the British treasury but also on British cultural legitimacy.

Gandhi claimed to have taken his concepts of nonviolence and civil disobedience from the British suffragists, who had chained themselves to the gates of Parliament in order to win the vote and who had gone on hunger strikes when jailed. His commitment to periodic fasting was meant to further his plans for an end to violent protests and hatred

between Hindus and Muslims. Like the hunger strikes of the suffragists, Gandhi's fasts had political effects both on his followers and on the authorities. Since then, the civil rights movement in the United States, as well as other liberation movements around the world, have found civil disobedience, noncooperation, and fasting to be useful political tools. In the following newspaper article, "My Loincloth" (1921), Gandhi explains why he has abandoned Western dress and taken up traditional Indian cloth and clothing.

I began telling people in my speeches: "If you don't get khadi [hand-spun cloth], you will do with mere loin-cloth but discard foreign clothing." But I know that I was hesitating whilst I uttered those words. They lacked the necessary force, as long as I had my dhoti and my shirt on.

The dearth of *swadeshi* [self-sufficiency] in Madras, also continued to make me uneasy. The people seemed to be overflowing with love but it appeared to be all froth. . . .

Thus we reached Madura [near Madras] on the night of the 22nd. I decided that I should content myself with only a loin-cloth until at least the 31st of October. I addressed a meeting of the Madura weavers early next morning in loin-cloth. Today is the third day. . . .

If India calls me a lunatic, what then? If the co-workers do not copy my example, what then? Of course this is not meant to be copied by co-workers. It is meant simply to hearten the people, and to make my way clear. Unless I went about with a loin-cloth, how might I advise others to do likewise? What should I do where millions have to go naked? . . .

I want the reader to measure from this the agony of my soul. I do not want either my co-workers or readers to adopt the loin-cloth. But I do wish that they should thoroughly realize the meaning of the boycott of foreign cloth and put forth their best effort to get it boycotted . . . . I do wish that they may understand that *swadeshi* means everything.

Movements for African liberation also escalated their attacks on imperialism in the context of World War I and its aftermath. People in Africa and of African heritage had been

IVORY & APES & PEACOCKS

East Africa. The land from which, men say, ages ago King Solomon's ships came sailing with their freight of rare and precious things, " gold and ivory, apes and peacocks."

To-day it is British—and of all the tropical domains of the Empire none is richer in promise than this vast territory twenty times the size of England. But to-day its wealth is of another kind. Coffee from the uplands of Uganda, Tanganyika and, above all, Kenya. Tobacco from Rhodesia and Nyasaland, which also sends us Tea. Cotton from Uganda. Sisal from Tanganyika and Kenya. Cloves from Zanzibar.

You have a personal interest in the future of East Africa. For as her new industries prosper, her orders for British goods grow larger year by year, and that means more employment and better times for all of us.

Drink Empire coffee—smoke Empire tobacco—use Empire binder twine. You'll be helping in one of the greatest colonising ventures to which the British race has ever set its hand.

EAST AFRICA
sends us
COFFEE—TEA—TOBACCO—COTTON—MAIZE
SISAL—HIDES & SKINS—CLOVES
COPRA—OILSEEDS—GUMS—BINDER TWINE

Issued by the Empire Marketing Board

After World War I, imperial powers became more dependent than ever on colonial trade and prosperity, as this advertisement urging British people to buy imperial goods shows.

combating each successive round of imperial oppression with the development of various political programs and spontaneous resistance to imperial occupation. Growing up before World War I, Pan-Africanism was a political movement that tried to unify Africans everywhere to address their special grievances. At first its leaders came from Africa itself, but soon activists appeared from every part of the world housing the African diaspora, or the populace dispersed from the African homeland. Prominent Pan-Africanists included the American philosopher, scholar, and political activist W. E. B. Du Bois. The movement's first meeting took place in London in 1900; another convened at the peace conference in Paris in 1919. The latter congress called on the victorious powers to act to end slavery and to protect African workers and resources. Finally, the 1921 congress issued a "Declaration to the World," also called the London Manifesto. Pan-Africanism has remained influential down to the present day.

The Suppressed Races through their thinking leaders are demanding:

1. The recognition of civilised men as civilised despite their race and colour.

2. Local self-government for backward groups, deliberately rising as experience and knowledge grow to complete self-government under the limitations of a self-governed world.

3. Education in self-knowledge, in scientific truth and in industrial technique, undivorced from the art of beauty.

4. Freedom in their own religion and customs and with the right to be non-conformist and different.

5. Co-operation with the rest of the world in government, industry and art on the basis of Justice, Freedom and Peace.

6. The ancient common ownership of the Land and its natural fruits and defence against the unrestrained greed of invested capital.

7. The establishment under the League of Nations of an international institution for the study of Negro problems.

8. The establishment of an international section of the Labour Bureau of the League of Nations, charged with the protection of native labour.

The world must face two eventualities; either the complete assimilation of Africa with two or three of the great world states, with political, civil and social power and privileges absolutely equal for its black and white citizens, or the rise of a great black

African State, founded in Peace and Good Will, based on popular education, natural art and industry and freedom of trade, autonomous and sovereign in its internal policy, but from its beginning a part of a great society of peoples in which it takes its place with others as co-rulers of the world.

In some such words and thoughts we seek to express our will and ideal and the end of our untiring effort. . . . The absolute equality of races, physical, political and social, is the founding stone of World Peace and human advancement. No one denies great differences of gift, capacity and attainment among individuals of all races, but the voice of Science, Religion and practical Politics is one in denying the God-appointed existence of super-races or of races naturally and inevitably inferior. . . .

The habit of democracy must be made to encircle the earth. Despite the attempt to prove that its practice is the secret and divine Gift of the Few, no habit is more natural and more widely-spread among primitive peoples or more easily capable of development among wide masses. . . .

Brewing and Shaming

Preparation for liberation took place in large public meetings and with the publication of grand statements of principles. It also occurred in more private ways as a result of imperialism's inroads on people's lives. One example comes from the brewing of beer in cities. Increasingly in the 20th century, imperialism led to the development of new cities for trade, industry, and government. As imperialism's economics forced people off the land, many moved to these new cities. Yet within the cities women maintained their old customs of rural life, such as brewing beer for their families but also for paying customers. However, many imperial regimes tried to monitor the production and distribution of alcohol simply for purposes of control, if not taxation. Just as they had earlier taxed salt and other commodities, the imperial authorities often made home brewing illegal, to gain more revenue from industrial producers.

In this passage taken from an oral interview, a South African woman, Mmadiate Makgale, describes her arrest for brewing in the years after World War I. Women's continued brewing despite being regularly arrested for it was a form of civil disobedience that laid the groundwork for more overtly political activism.

"Throughout the world there had been opposition, a disposition not to treat civilised negroes as civilised, a disposition to consider that negro races existed in the world chiefly for the benefit of white races, a disposition to draw colour lines and race lines. All these things together, apart from the problems in the particular countries constituted a world problem. They had begun to see more or less dimly there was in the world an international problem and they had got to talk about it."

—W. E. B. Du Bois, 1921

Films of the 1920s and 1930s such as
Sanders of the River *took up the colonial theme, contrasting white and black, power and powerlessness for Western audiences. Viewers flocked to such movies, which were fictional dramas set in China, the Middle East, and Africa.*

My husband, who was fond of behaving like an Englishman, stood up, went to the door, and said, "Somebody is knocking at the door, he says I must open the door." He went to the door but the person who was holding the calabash in his hand persuaded him not to open the door before he could finish that beer. My husband refused to wait for some time. He opened the door, and with lightning speed, the policeman pushed my husband aside and went straight to the man who was holding the calabash in his hand. . . . The man said, "Your husband did a foolish mistake to open the door knowing that it is the policeman who is knocking at the door." I was arrested for the first time in my life.

My firstborn, who I said was mentally handicapped, rushed to one woman I was related to . . . and made her aware that I had been arrested so that she could hide whatever liquor she had. She said she took the calabash full of beer immediately and threw it away. . . .

The policeman asked whether I was being arrested for the first time because they could see that I was not used to it. When we arrived at the police station my husband and some other people arrived a few minutes later. . . . We left the police station after he had paid the fine. . . .

What angered me most was that when asked by the police whether I had brewed beer for selling, he agreed with them. I tried to deny it, arguing that I had brewed it for his consumption and not for sale. So, whenever he asked for home-brewed beer, I would refuse to do it. . . . I would say, "You disappointed me before whites at the police station, I have no hope in you. You tell those whites that I have brewed beer for sale because you were afraid of arrest."

In 1929, groups of women living in southeastern Nigeria dressed themselves up in war attire of loincloths and wreaths of palms. They rubbed their faces with charcoal and ashes and set out for the Native Administration buildings. The troubles stemmed from the British government's widening attempts to standardize taxation on all the inhabitants of the provinces. Women, whose traditional income from palm oil had been declining, feared that their livelihood

would be affected, because officials started inventorying their homes and assessing their goods. Moreover, the British practice of selecting local leaders for governance violated the ground rules that several ethnic groups observed when it came to selecting leaders. Women saw "warfare"—the practices of ritual chanting, singing, and ridiculing—as their legitimate response to an intensifying colonialism. To the British way of interpreting local politics, these were "savage riots" in which women were egged on by men. But to the thousands involved it was exclusively a women's "war"—one involving women's long-standing practices of resistance. Here are their demands as they were presented to the government, along with their vehement denial that they were acting as anything but their own agents.

1. The Government will not tax women.

2. No personal property, such as boxes, is to be counted.

3. Any one woman who is a known prostitute is [not] to be arrested.

4. Women are not to be charged rent for the use of the common market shed.

5. They ask that licenses for holding plays should not be paid for.

6. They do not want Chief Mark Pepple to be Head Chief of Obopo Town.

7. The women do not want any man to pay tax.

8. They are speaking for Obopo, Bonny and Andoni women.

It has been suggested here that men encouraged women to move about. I deny that statement. It is not true. We were not encouraged by men. . . . It is against native custom for women to leave their houses without permission of their husbands but in this case men had been made to pay tax and the rumor that women were going to be taxed was spread around. Women became infuriated because they had already felt the burden of the tax on men . . . . We acted according to our own consciences. . . . The matter did not concern men.

Global Mixture Continues

Although Gandhi and others built their protests around the rejection of Western culture, the customs of imperialists—now including more radical changes such as coeducation—continued to be accepted as signs of modernity. After the

Claiming to befriend the local subjects of her studies, American anthropologist Margaret Mead—one of the most celebrated scholars of "primitive" people—wears native clothing conspicuously in an undeveloped environment. Anthropology and ethnography gained academic status during the interwar years, and Mead's books were all the rage in skyscraper-lined cities of the United States.

Veiling and Unveiling

Veiling women's faces has been a custom in many regions for at least two millennia. Like the seclusion of women in special quarters of a house, the custom has had several meanings, including the guarantee of women's privacy and sexual purity and the expression of religious faith. Wealthy and middle-income families were most likely to make their women veil themselves, while women in peasant or working families and people in rural areas often went unveiled. Thus in 19th- and early 20th-century Egypt, for example, Christian, Jewish, and Muslim women from wealthy homes were the ones who veiled themselves. In those days it was not a custom connected with religion so much as with class and status, whereas unveiling in the early 20th century was meant to symbolize national and personal liberation for colonized peoples.

partition of much of the former Ottoman Empire under the mandate system, Mustafa Kemal established the Turkish republic in 1923 from the core region of the old empire around Istanbul. He built the new nation around a detailed program of Westernization that made Western dress mandatory and outlawed polygamy, the practice of having more than one wife (Islamic law permitted men to have multiple wives). In this and many other nationalist movements women had changed their regional dress for Western attire to support independence, and some lobbied for the improved legal position of women, but such changes were jarring.

Coeducation also disturbed the traditional practice of segregating the sexes. It took time to work out all the embarrassment and awkwardness of such a new way of doing things. Badr ol-Moluk Bamdad, among the first women admitted to Tehran University, provides this account of her first days there.

While the girls had deliberately and prudently prepared themselves for entry, the boys were completely disconcerted. For most of them, mixing with girls was something quite unforeseen. They therefore avoided talking to the girls or even answering them, and if there was no escape they blushed from ear to ear and stuttered. At the lectures, wherever a girl sat, the bench on each side of her stayed empty.

Certain elderly professors were just as nervous as the boy students about speaking to girls and looking them in the face. One girl, then in her second year at the university, asked a professor who had shut his eyes when replying to a question from her, "Don't you trust your eyes, professor?" He was puzzled and asked, "What do you mean?" "I mean why won't you look at the girls?"

As for the librarian, the sight of the girls side by side with the boys disturbed him so much that he marked off a special corner like a harem where the girls might safely sit.

In the 18th century, Japan began learning intensively about European medicine from the Dutch. In its quest to become a great, modern power, in the late 19th century the government imported many Western physicians, especially German ones. A fine Japanese novel about Japan between the two world wars shows its upper-class characters regularly giving themselves vitamin B shots for energy. Yet these Western ways were losing some of their luster, because its imperial

The International Colonial Exposition in Paris in 1931 was one of the last great celebrations of imperial power. But while the French celebrated, protestors produced tracts showing an imprisoned Africa being beaten by officials and soldiers. Anti-imperial movements had infiltrated the colonial powers.

Publications Issued by the Official French Tourist Office French Government

Edition de l'Office Algérien d'Action Economique et Touristique du Gouvernement Général de l'Algérie
═══════════ 26, Boulevard Carnot - ALGER

At the time of this advertisement for Algerian tourism, cigarettes were considered fashionable, and advertisers used them to symbolize sophistication. Whereas 19th-century travel was promoted for educational reasons, 20th-century tourism made a person sophisticated and smart.

triumphs made Japan look to its Asian past, reviving, for example, such traditional practices as acupuncture, homeopathy, and moxa cures (using wormwood as a cauterizing agent for injured skin). What is more, during these years the West changed its own attitude toward medicine, with some European physicians advocating these ancient Chinese techniques. In the introduction to a medical book, French doctor Soulié de Mourant endorsed for his European colleagues the work of the Japanese doctor T. Nakayama on acupuncture and moxa cures. Showing the continuing and complex cultural mixtures of the day, Nakayama himself describes the debate in Japan over Eastern versus Western medicine.

Dr. Soulié de Mourant: Having mastered the Western medical method, the corps of Japanese doctors came to disagree bit by bit. Some, without having studied Chinese medicine, rejected it out of hand because Europeans didn't know about it. Others were not able to close their eyes to the sometimes miraculous cures effected by the practitioners of the old Chinese method. . . .

Among the doctors whose education kept them aware of the reality of the facts, a certain number asked whether it wouldn't be useful to study all the effects of Chinese medicine, either by needles, moxas, or homeopathy.

For years these learned men have made innumerable experiments either treating the sick in clinics and hospitals through observation, bloodtests, and various analyses, etc. or in experimenting on animals that one killed to determine the results. . . .

The mocking depiction of tango dancers on this sheet-music cover chastises conservatives who tended to attribute all social ills to foreign influence. "Right, it's the tango that makes him crazy," the song goes. The popular culture of Africa, Asia, and Latin America heavily influenced dances and popular music by the interwar years.

Their conclusions will perhaps shock those Westerners who think we have reached the heights of progress and who are convinced that what they have studied has nothing to teach other methods or peoples.

Nonetheless the very principles of our medical predecessors have many times been shown wrong [by their studies]. Only the most solid remain valid. . . .

Dr. Nakayama: Is it possible that the old Chinese medicine is really a science? That is a troubling question. It has, for the modern person, nothing scientific. To the contrary it is covered with a mysterious prehistoric patina and seems even incomprehensible. Nonetheless, one can hardly ignore it when one hears of its remarkable therapeutic effectiveness. . . .

Chinese medicine is above all superior to that of the West in terms of its physical therapeutic by means of needles and moxas, a therapeutic dating from prehistoric times but extremely practical, even for Europeans.

It is independent of and at the same time complementary to medicine involving medication. One can use it without any knowledge of the theory of yin and yang, although this theory is a powerful tool. It is simple in principle and in practice, and thus accessible to everyone.

Its effectiveness is such that it is difficult even to imagine it. It is inexpensive, demands neither exceptional dexterity nor complicated, dangerous or clumsy apparatus nor a special installation. It does not inject toxins into the body. . . .

We are providing, among other things, graphs and tables made by colleagues to give a general and clear picture of the effect of moxas. They will show [us] in a way called "scientific" the efficacy of this [Chinese] method.

But to tell the truth, some Orientals do not blindly accept the Western method called "scientific." We are not ready to accept it entirely and this is because of our traditional education, which, for thousands of years has given us other means to judge fairly this so-called science and which leads us to consider all pure and empirical "scientific" method as too simplistic and almost infantile. . . .

The European saying "the exception proves the rule" appears to us a serious logical mistake. And we have seen too often in studying history that European science dismisses facts that don't fit with its current theories. Our medicine by contrast always tries to escape the uncertainties of knowledge with innumerable important experiments. . . . Chinese and Far Eastern medicine in truth is

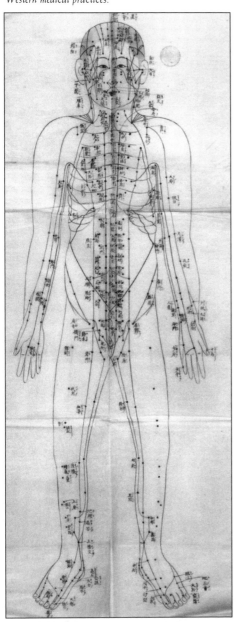

A Japanese diagram illustrates pressure points for acupuncture, a method of healing by sticking needles into the skin. Asian medicine proposed an increasingly popular alternative to Western medical practices.

the crystallization of observations and experiments pursued for millennia by a third of the human race. . . .

Fusion for Liberation

The ideas that shaped liberation movements could also depend on the prevalent cultural mixture, with all the complexities that mixture entailed. In the 19th century, reform movements in India, Egypt, and other colonized regions adopted Western notions of nationalism and equal rights. After the Russian Revolution of 1917 the Communism that arose provided an alternative set of political ideas to those originating in France or Britain. In particular, Communism (the name Lenin gave to his socialist movement after it had triumphed in Russia) stressed an end to private property, a more equal distribution of wealth, and the political ideal of international brotherhood rather than nationalism.

In China a communist movement under the revolutionary leader Mao Zedong gained a large following in the 1920s and 1930s with its appeals to struggle and its promises of a fairer distribution of property and goods. Another East Asian communist, Ho Chi Minh, who had been educated in Paris, founded the Communist Party of Indochina that would eventually stave off both French and U.S. attempts to maintain control of the area after World War II. Here is his founding manifesto to the Indochinese, one that differs from manifestos by the pan-Arab, pan-African, and other liberation movements. Using the Western rhetoric of Communism, his

treatise alludes to the severe repression by the French of independence movements in the region and to the increased need to make economic gains there.

Workers, peasants, soldiers, youth, and pupils!
Oppressed and exploited compatriots!
Sisters and brothers! Comrades!

Imperialist contradictions were the cause of the 1914–18 World War. After this horrible slaughter, the world was divided into two camps: One is the revolutionary camp including the oppressed colonies and the exploited working class throughout the world. The vanguard force of this camp is the Soviet Union. The other is the counterrevolutionary camp of international capitalism and imperialism whose general staff is the League of Nations.

During this World War, various nations suffered untold losses in property and human lives. The French imperialists were the hardest hit. Therefore, in order to restore the capitalist forces in France, the French imperialists have resorted to every underhand scheme to intensify their capitalist exploitation in Indochina. They set up new factories to exploit the workers with low wages. They plundered the peasants' land to establish plantations and drive them to utter poverty. They levied many heavy taxes. They imposed public loans upon our people. In short, they reduced us to wretchedness. . . .

This is the reason why the Vietnamese revolutionary movement has grown even stronger with each passing day. The workers refuse to work, the peasants demand land, the pupils strike, the traders boycott. Everywhere the masses have risen to oppose the French imperialists.

The Vietnamese revolution has made the French imperialists tremble with fear. . . They terrorize, arrest, jail, deport, and kill a great number of Vietnamese revolutionaries. . . .

The Communist Party of Indochina is founded. It is the party of the working class. . . . From now on we must join the Party, help it and follow it in order to implement the following slogans:

1. To overthrow French imperialism, feudalism, and the reactionary Vietnamese capitalist class.

For centuries Kurds have fought to establish their own nation. After the end of World War I and the fall of the Ottoman Empire, they were thwarted yet again when Iraq, Syria, and Turkey divided up Kurdish lands.

2. To make Indochina completely independent.

3. To establish a worker-peasant and soldier government.

4. To confiscate the banks and other enterprises belonging to the imperialists and put them under the control of the worker-peasant and soldier government.

5. To confiscate the whole of the plantations and property belonging to the imperialists and the Vietnamese reactionary capitalist class and distribute them to poor peasants.

6. To implement the eight-hour working day.

7. To abolish public loans and poll tax. To waive unjust taxes hitting the poor people.

8. To bring back all freedoms to the masses.

9. To carry out universal education.

10. To implement equality between man and woman.

Japan, the Eastern imperial power, used the language of anti-imperialism to build its empire further. By the 1930s Western imperialism was under severe pressure to reform, especially in Asia. The British were forced to acknowledge Egyptian independence, Gandhi made a celebrated visit to England. Japan rode the tide of anti-Western and liberationist feeling. Suffering economically from the Depression, Japan stiffened its imperial resolve. Groups of intellectuals and military men called for their country to throw off Western ways and expand Japan's mission in Asia. The result was the seizure of Manchuria in 1931, the outbreak of war with China in 1937, and finally entry into World War II in 1941 against the United States, Britain, and the Soviet Union. Japan built its empire in part on the rhetoric of an Asia free from an imperialist West. In these documents Japanese politicians call for their people to rethink the issue of Western influence and to expand the empire in the name of Asian development. In a 1937 book, *Fundamentals of Our National Polity*, the ministry of education questioned Japan's admiration for Western ideas on which the Meiji Restoration reform government of 1868 had been based.

The various ideological and social evils of present-day Japan are . . . due to the fact that since the days of Meiji so many aspects of European and American culture, systems, and learning, have been imported, and that, too rapidly. . . . [T]he present conflict seen in our people's ideas, the unrest of their modes of life, the confused state of their civilization, can be put right only by a thorough investigation by us of the intrinsic nature of Occidental ideologies and by grasping the true meaning of our national polity. Then, too, this should be done not only for the sake of our nation but for the sake of the entire human race. . . .

The politician Hashimoto Kingorō, in "The Need for Emigration and Expansion," justified expansion in terms that captured the population boom in Asia since World War I.

We have already said that there are only three ways left to Japan to escape from the pressure of surplus population. We are like a great crowd of people packed into a small and narrow room, and there are only three doors through which we might escape, namely emigration, advance into world markets, and expansion of territory. The first door, emigration, has been barred to us by anti-Japanese immigration policies of other countries. The second door, advance into world markets, is being pushed shut by tariff barriers and the abrogation of commercial treaties. What should Japan do when two of the three doors have been closed against her?

It is quite natural that Japan should rush upon the last remaining door.

It may sound dangerous when we speak of territorial expansion, but the territorial expansion of which we speak does not in any sense of the word involve the occupation of the possessions of other countries, the planting of the Japanese flag thereon, and the declaration of their annexation to Japan. It is just that since the Powers have suppressed the circulation of Japanese materials and merchandise abroad, we are looking for some place overseas where Japanese capital, Japanese skills, and Japanese labor can have free play, free from oppression of the white race. . . .

And if it is still protested that our actions in Manchuria were excessively violent, we may wish to ask the white race just which country it was that sent warships and troops to India, South Africa, and Australia and slaughtered innocent natives, bound their hands and feet with iron chains, lashed their backs with iron whips, proclaimed these territories as their own, and still continues to hold them to this very day?

They will invariably reply, these were all lands inhabited by untamed savages. These people did not know how to develop the abundant resources of their land for the benefit of mankind. Therefore it was the wish of God, who created heaven and earth for mankind, for us to develop these undeveloped lands and to promote the happiness of mankind in their stead. God wills it.

In 1937 Japanese troops invaded Shanghai, China's most important harbor. Japan justified its move as necessary to bring about the liberation of Asian peoples from Western imperialism. In fact, the Japanese set out to claim natural resources in Asia in order to further develop their industrial and military power.

This is quite a convenient argument for them. Let us take it at face value. Then there is another question we must ask them.

Suppose that there is still on this earth land endowed with abundant natural resources that have not been developed at all by the white race. Would it not then be God's will and the will of Providence that Japan go there and develop those resources for the benefit of mankind?

And here is Tokutomi Iichirō, in his *Commentary on the Imperial Declaration of War:*

Now that we have risen up in arms, we must accomplish our aim to the last. Herein lies the core of our theory. In Nippon resides a destiny to become the Light of Greater East Asia and to become ultimately the Light of the World. . . . [T]o become the Light of Greater East Asia, we must have three qualifications. The first is, as mentioned previously, strength. In other words, we must expel Anglo-Saxon influence from East Asia with our strength.

To speak the truth, the various races of East Asia look upon the British and Americans as superior to the Nippon race. Therefore, we must show our real strength before all our fellow-races of East Asia. We must show them an object lesson. It is not a lesson in words. It should be a lesson in facts.

In other words, before we can expel the Anglo-Saxons and make them remove all their traces from East Asia, we must annihilate them. In this way only will the various fellow races of Greater East Asia look upon us as their leader. . . .

The second qualification is benevolence. Nippon must develop the various resources of East Asia and distribute them fairly to all the races within the East Asia Co-Prosperity Sphere to make them share in the benefits. In other words, Nippon should not monopolize the benefits but should distribute them for the mutual prosperity of Greater East Asia. . . .

The third qualification is virtue. East Asia embraces various races. Its religions are different. Moreover, there has practically been no occasion when these have mutually united to work for a combined aim. It was the favorite policy of the Anglo-Saxons to make the various races of East Asia compete and fight each other and make them mutually small and powerless. We must, therefore, console them, bring friendship among them, and make them all live in peace with a boundlessly embracing virtue.

Epilogue

All the imperialist nations claimed to be benefiting those they conquered and oppressed. In this regard Japan was no different from the United States justifying its conquest of the Philippines or the great European powers plundering the African and Asian continents. The difference is that the Japanese expansion of the 1930s and early 1940s proved to be the final blow to the age of high imperialism that had begun in the 19th century. Where it did not destroy the European grasp, Japanese conquest weakened it. It contributed to the general catastrophe of World War II that spread so much disorder globally. When the war ended, empires collapsed.

Despite its disintegration after World War II, imperialism as a system of direct political rule of conquered areas left an enduring legacy. It had truly internationalized commerce and politics because of the systems of rapid transportation and communication embodied in the railroad, steamship, telegraph, and telephone involved in imperialism's triumph. In these circumstances Western culture lost the distinctiveness that it might have retained from Europe's relative isolation. Instead, Western civilization became a culture profoundly dependent on taking and incorporating ideas, customs, and resources from the rest of the world. Although there was a great deal of borrowing in the other direction as well, some have argued that imperialism had far less effect outside the West in cultural terms. Instead, the real effect of imperialism elsewhere was in its plunder and rapacious devastation of resources, whether that plundering was committed by the English, Belgians, Russians, Americans, or Japanese. To some extent, that devastation made traditional family ties, religion, customs, and ways of living more prized than ever before, despite—and perhaps because of—the difficulty of maintaining them.

Another legacy of imperialism is the incredible and increasing global violence that has since the 19th century killed hundreds of millions in colonial conquest and forced labor, world wars, wars of liberation, and civil wars—all of them connected in one way or another to imperialism and its aftermath. It is one of imperialism's

After China deposed its imperial family just before World War I, a new culture emerged touting Western ways. Footwear such as Keds shoes appeared on billboards, and the new government promoted Western habits such as cleaning the teeth with a brush. Despite the drive to improve everyday life, it remained arduous in the late 1920s.

many paradoxes that while it made people more aware than ever before of the world's multiple races, accomplishments, and cultures, it set a trend of pitting humans against one another in an orgy of conquest, competition, and hatred. Yet at the same time, around the globe population soared, health improved, technology became more modern, and concern for human rights advanced.

A final legacy and paradox of imperialism is that its end saw the world increasingly divided between prosperous peoples of the former imperial powers and poorer peoples who had once been colonized. Differences in wealth became greater, and a new or neo-imperialism had replaced the old. This neo-imperialism was one based—as it had been before political conquest in the 19th century—on trading superiority and on a culture of curiosity, acquisitiveness, and conquest. Although the age of high imperialism ended long ago, it continues to shape our present world.

Timeline

1500s–1700s

European colonial and trade expansion; Asian and African traders and explorers expand their outposts

1600s

Coffee, tea, chocolate, and other products become global commodities and enter the European diet

1700s

Art, architecture, gardening, technical procedures, and ideas borrowed by the West and Japan from China; wars for colonial territory primarily among the British and French

1791

Slave uprising in Saint Domingue

1794

French National Convention abolishes slavery in the colonies

1804

Republic of Haiti declared

1830

France begins conquest of Algeria

1839

Outbreak of opium wars between China and Britain

1840s–90s

Russian expansion into Central and West Asia

1857

Sepoy Rebellion in India

1869

Suez Canal opens

1870s–present

Modern art and music adopt Asian and African motifs

1876

Queen Victoria becomes Empress of India

1879

Partition of West Africa begins

1880s

Germany takes parts of East Africa

1882

British invade and take control of Egypt

1884–85

European nations carve up Africa at Berlin Conference

1885

Indian National Congress founded

1885–86

British annex Burma

1887

France creates Union of Indochina

1890s
Partition of East Africa

1890s–1914
Increasing rebellion and political activism in Africa and Asia against colonial powers

1894
Sino-Japanese War

1898
U.S. defeats Spain, annexes Philippines

1898–1901
Boer War

1900
Boxer Rebellion in China

1900–14
Uprisings against imperial powers across Africa

1904–5
Russo-Japanese War

1908
Young Turks take over government in Constantinople

1910
Japan annexes Korea; Union of South Africa established

1911–12
Chinese reformers overthrow the Qing dynasty; China becomes a republic

1914–18
Asian and African soldiers fight in World War I

1919
Peace of Paris dismantles German empire and institutes mandate system; Amritsar Massacre in India

1920s–30s
Mohandas Gandhi leads a mass independence movement in India

1923
Turkey becomes a republic and Mustafa Kemal begins policy of westernization

1929
Women's War in Nigeria

1930s
Ho Chi Minh builds Indochinese socialist party aiming for independence

1931
Japan invades Manchuria

1936
Britain grants Egypt self rule

1937
Japan invades China

1939–45
World War II; loosening of imperial control; Asian and African troops play important role; Japan loses its colonial possessions

1947
Indian Independence

1950s and 1960s
African and Asian colonies achieve independence

1990s
Much of Russian empire becomes independent

1997
Britain returns Hong Kong to China

Further Reading

Adas, Michael. *"High" Imperialism and the "New" History.* Washington, D.C.: American Historical Association, 1993.

————. *Machines as the Measure of Men: Science, Technology, and Ideologies of Western Dominance.* Ithaca, N.Y.: Cornell University Press, 1989.

Adeloye, Adelola. *African Pioneers of Modern Medicine: Nigerian Doctors of the Nineteenth Century.* Ibadan, Nigeria: University Press, 1985.

Baumgart, Winfred. *Imperialism: The Idea and Reality of British and French Colonial Expansion, 1880–1914.* New York: Oxford University Press, 1982.

Beckles, Hilary McD. *Liberation Cricket: West Indies Cricket Culture.* Manchester, England: Manchester University Press, 1995.

Blakely, Allison. *Blacks in the Dutch World: The Evolution of Racial Imagery in Modern Society.* Bloomington: Indiana University Press, 1993.

Bozzoli, Belinda. *Women of Phokeng: Consciousness, Life Strategy, and Migrancy in South Africa, 1900–1983.* London: Heinemann, 1991.

Chaudhuri, Nupur, and Margaret Strobel, eds. *Western Women and Imperialism: Complicity and Resistance.* Bloomington: Indiana University Press, 1992.

Clarke, J. J. *Oriental Enlightenment: The Encounter between Asian and Western Thought.* London: Routledge, 1997.

Crosby, Alfred. *Imperialism: The Biological Expansion of Europe 900–1900.* New York: Cambridge University Press, 1986.

Flint, John E. *Sir George Goldie and the Making of Nigeria.* London: Oxford University Press, 1960.

Gailey, Harry A. *The Road to Aba: A Study of British Administrative Policy in Eastern Nigeria.* New York: New York University Press, 1970.

Gates, Barbara T. *Kindred Nature: Victorian and Edwardian Women Embrace the Living World.* Chicago: University of Chicago Press, 1998.

Giffard, Sydney. *Japan Among the Powers, 1890–1990.* New Haven: Yale University Press, 1994.

Headrick, Daniel. *The Tentacles of Progress: Technology Transfer in the Age of Imperialism, 1850–1940.* New York: Oxford University Press, 1988.

Hobsbawm, Eric. *The Age of Empire, 1875–1914.* New York: Pantheon, 1987.

Hyam, Ronald. *Empire and Sexuality: The British Experience.* Manchester, England: Manchester University Press, 1990.

Knoll, Arthur J., and Lewis H. Gann, eds. *Germans in the Tropics: Essays in German Colonial History.* New York: Greenwood, 1987.

Koponen, Juhani. *Development for Exploitation: German Colonial Policies in Mainland Tanzania, 1884–1914.* Helsinki: Finnish Historical Society, 1995.

Kuitenbrouwer, Maarten. *The Netherlands and the Rise of Modern Imperialism.* Hugh Beyer, trans. New York: Berg, 1991.

Lebovics, Herman. *True France: The Wars over Cultural Identity, 1900–1940.* Ithaca, N.Y.: Cornell University Press, 1992.

MacKenzie, John. *The Empire of Nature: Hunting, Conservation, and British Imperialism.* Manchester, England: Manchester University Press, 1988.

Mangan, J. A. *The Games Ethic and Imperialism: Aspects of the Diffusion of an Ideal.* New York: Viking, 1986.

Manning, Ralph R. *The Art of the Possible: Documents on Great Power Diplomacy, 1814–1914.* New York: McGraw-Hill, 1996.

Mintz, Sidney W. *Sweetness and Power: The Place of Sugar in Modern History.* New York: Penguin, 1985.

Mitter, Partha. *Much Maligned Monsters: A History of European Reactions to Indian Art.* Chicago: University of Chicago Press, 1992.

Morris-Suzuki, Tessa. *The Technological Transformation of Japan from the Seventeenth to the Twenty-first Century.* New York: Cambridge University Press, 1994.

Mudimbe, V. Y. *The Idea of Africa.* Bloomington: Indiana University Press, 1994.

Myers, Ramon, and Mark R. Peattie. *The Japanese Colonial Empire, 1895–1945.* Princeton, N.J.: Princeton University Press, 1984.

Sangari, Kumkum, and Sudeshi Vaid, eds. *Recasting Women: Essays in Indian Colonial History.* New Brunswick, N.J.: Rutgers University Press, 1990.

Shillington, Kevin. *History of Africa.* New York: Macmillan, 1989.

Wesseling, H. L. *Divide and Rule: The Partition of Africa, 1880–1914.* Arnold J. Pomerans, trans. Westport, Conn.: Praeger, 1996.

White, Luise. *The Comforts of Home: Prostitution in Colonial Nairobi.* Chicago: University of Chicago Press, 1990.

Yergin, Daniel. *The Prize: The Epic Quest for Oil, Money, and Power.* New York: Simon & Schuster, 1991.

Text Credits

Main Text

pp. 19–20: Lady Mary Wortley Montagu. Letter to Mrs. Thistlethwayte, April 1, 1717. In *The Letters and Works of Lady Mary Wortley Montagu*. Ed. Lord Wharncliffe. 2 vols. 1861. Reprint. New York: AMS Press, 1970, 310.

pp. 21–22: André Michaux. Letter to André Thouin, July 30, 1782. In *André and François Michaux*. Ed. Henry Savage. Charlottesville: University Press of Virginia, 1986, 17.

pp. 21–22: André Michaux. Letter to Monsieur, brother of the king, January 14, 1783. In Savage, 24–25.

pp. 22–23: Quoted in Bernard Lewis, *The Muslim Discovery of Europe*. New York: Norton, 1982, 288.

pp. 23–24: Morishima Chūryō quoted in Donald Keene, *The Japanese Discovery of Europe, 1720–1830*. Stanford: Stanford University Press, 1969, 70.

p. 25: Li Shih-Yao, "Five Rules to Regulate Foreigners," 1759. In *China in Transition, 1517–1911*. Ed. Dun J. Li. New York: Van Nostrand Reinhold, 1969, 29–31.

p. 26: *Algemeen Huishoudelijk-, Natuur-, Zedekundig- en Konst-Woordenboek*. Leiden, Netherlands: Joh. le Mair, 1778. Quoted in Allison Blakely, *Blacks in the Dutch World: The Evolution of Racial Imagery in Modern Society*. Bloomington: Indiana University Press, 1993, 34. Copyright © Indiana University Press, 1993.

pp. 27–28: Lynn Hunt, ed. and trans. *The French Revolution and Human Rights. A Brief Documentary History*. Boston: Bedford Books of St. Martin's Press, 1996, 109, 111.

pp. 28–29: Henri Christophe to Commandant Vilton. Letter 20 Germinal Year 10. In *Haytian Papers. A Collection of the Very Interesting Proclamations and Other Official Documents Together with Some Account of the Rise, Progress, and Present State of the Kingdom of Hayti*. Ed. Prince Sanders. Boston: Caleb Bingham, 1818, 43–44, 49.

p. 30: Simon Bolívar, "On the Policy of England," *Gaceta de Caracas*, February 7, 1814. In *Selected Writings of Bolívar*. Ed. Harold A. Bierck, trans. Lewis Bertrand, 2 vols. New York: Colonial Press, 1951, 1:70–71.

p. 31: James Monroe, "The Monroe Doctrine," December 2, 1823. Quoted in *James Monroe, 1758–1831: Chronology—Documents—Bibliographical Aids*. Ed. Ian Elliot. Dobbs Ferry, N.Y.: Oceana Publications, 1969, 68–69.

pp. 35–36: Huang Chüeh-Tz'u, "The Evil of Opium," 1838. In *China in Transition: 1517–1911*. Ed. Dun J. Li. New York: Van Nostrand Reinhold Co., 1969, 54–55.

pp. 37–39: "The Queen's Proclamation to the Princes, Chiefs, and People of India," November 1, 1858. In *Readings in the Constitutional History of India, 1757–1947*. Delhi: Oxford University Press, 1983, 299–300. Reprinted by arrangement with Oxford University Press, India.

pp. 39–41: Evelyn Baring, Earl of Cromer, *Modern Egypt*. 2 vols. New York: Macmillan, 1908, I:4–6; II:146–48.

pp. 42–43: Edward Hertslet, *The Map of Europe by Treaty*. 4 vols. London: Butterworths, 1875–91, II:468–87.

pp. 43–45: "Royal Charter Granted to the National African Company," 1886. Quoted in John E. Flint, *Sir George Goldie and the Making of Nigeria*. London: Oxford University Press, 1960, 330–35.

p. 45: "Prince Aleksandr Mikhailovich Gorchakov." In *Source Book for Russian History from Early Times to 1917*. Ed. George Vernadsky et al. 3 vols. New Haven, Conn.: Yale University Press, 1972, III: 610.

pp. 46–47: Ernst Constans, "Debate in Chamber of Deputies," November 20, 1888. In Jules Ferry, *Le Tonkin et la mère-patrie*. Trans. B.G. Smith. Paris: Victor-Havard, 1890, 120–21, 289.

p. 48: Saigō Takamori. Letter to Itagaki, July 29, 1873. Quoted in *Sources of Japanese Tradition*. Ed. Ryusaku Tsunoda, William Theodore de Bary, and Donald Keene. New York: Columbia University Press, 1958, 655–56.

p. 49: Morinosuke Kajima, ed., *The Diplomacy of Japan, 1894–1922*. Tokyo: Kajima Institute, 1976, 104.

pp. 50–51: Mildred S. Wertheimer, *The Pan-German League*. New York: Columbia University Press, 1924, 95, 106–8.

pp. 52: "Message of President Harrison Transmitting Treaty of Annexation," February 13, 1893. In Henry Steele Commager, *Documents of American History*. 9th ed., 2 vols. Englewood Cliffs, N.J.: Prentice-Hall, 1973, 1:602–3.

p. 53: "Cleveland's Withdrawal of the Treaty for Annexation of Hawaii," 1893. In Commager (1973): 1:603–4.

p. 59: In Daniel R. Headrick, *The Tentacles of Progress: Technology Transfer in the Age of Imperialism, 1850–1940*. New York: Oxford University Press, 1988, 210.

p. 60: Rev. J. B. Murphy in *Times* (London), November 18, 1895. In Kevin Shillington, *History of Africa*. London: Macmillan, 1989, 334–36.

pp. 60–61: Charles Gide, "A quoi servent les colonies," *Revue de Géographie*, October 15, 1885. In Charles-Robert Ageron, *L'anticolonialisme en France de 1871 à 1914*. Trans. B.G. Smith. Paris: Presses Universitaires de France, 1973, 45–46. © PUF, Paris, 1973.

pp. 62–64: Mary Grant Seacole, *Wonderful Adventures of Mrs. Seacole in Many Lands*. New York: Oxford University Press, 1988, 61, 62–63, 76, 77, 120, 166–67.

p. 65: Sosrokartono, 1899 speech. Quoted in A.B. Lapian, "Indonesian Perceptions of the Colonial Power," in H.L. Wesseling, *Divide and Rule: The Partition of Africa, 1880–1914*. Trans. Arnold J. Pomerans. Westport, Conn.: Praeger, 1996, 84.

p. 66: "Lettre d'un commerçant de Nam-Dinh a la Société de géographie commercial, fevrier 1883." In Jules Ferry, *Le Tonkin et la mère-patrie: Témoignages et documents*. Trans. B. G. Smith. Paris: Victor-Havard, 1890, 298–99.

p. 67: In *Colonial Rule in Africa: Readings from Primary Sources*. Ed. Bruce Fetter. Madison: University of Wisconsin Press, 1979, 117.

pp. 68–69: In Charles Lee Keeton, *King Thebaw and the Ecological Rape of Burma. The Political and Commercial Struggle Between British India and French Indo-China in Burma 1878–1886*. Delhi: Manohar Book Service, 1974, 200–1, 202, 240, 347.

pp. 69–71: *Young Winston's Wars. The Original Despatches of Winston S. Churchill, War Correspondent, 1897–1900*. Ed. Frederick Woods. London: Leo Cooper, 1973, 98, 100, 101, 102, 103, 105, 107, 114. Reproduced with permission of Curtis Brown Ltd, London, on behalf of Winston S. Churchill. Copyright Winston S. Churchill 1992.

p. 72: "Dr. Dellys, report in Archives d'Outre-Mer." In Yvonne Turin, *Affrontements culturels dans l'algérie coloniale*. 2nd ed. Trans. B. G. Smith. Algiers, Algeria: Entreprise nationale du livre, 1971, 318–19.

p. 73: Dr. A. R. Cook, *Uganda Memories*. 1900. In Luise White, " 'They Could Make Their Victims Dull': Genders and Genres, Fantasies and Cures in Colonial Southern Uganda," *American Historical Review* (December 1995): 1,386.

p. 73: In Adelola Adeloye, *African Pioneers of Modern Medicine. Nigerian Doctors of the Nineteenth Century*. Ibadan, Nigeria: University Press, 1985, 69–70.

pp. 77–78: J.E.C. Welldon, "The Imperial Purpose of Education," in *Proceedings of the Royal Colonial Institute* XXVI (1894–95), 829; J.E.C. Welldon, *Forty Years On*. London: Nicholson and Watson, 1935, 140, 262.

p. 79: William Cotton Oswell, in John M. MacKenzie, *The Empire of Nature: Hunting, Conservation, and British Imperialism*. Manchester, England: Manchester University Press, 1988, 101.

pp. 79–80: Kate Martelli, *Tigers I Have Shot*. In Joanna Trollope, *Britannia's Daughters: Women of the British Empire*. London: Hutchinson, 1983, 207.

p. 80: Frederick Jackson, in MacKenzie, 162; Richard Meinertzhagen, in MacKenzie, 158–59.

p. 80: Sir Frederick Lugard, in MacKenzie, 157.

pp. 81–82: Margaret Fountaine, *Love Among the Butterflies*. New York: Penguin, 1980, 119, 120, 125.

pp. 83–84: Sir Frederick Lugard, "Report on the Amalgamation of Northern and Southern Nigeria," (1919) quoted in Mahmood Mamdani, *Citizen and Subject. Contemporary Africa and the Legacy of Late Colonialism*. Princeton: Princeton University Press, 1996, 78–79.

pp. 84–85: Quoted in Hafeez Malik, *Sir Sayyid Ahmad Khan and Muslim Modernization in India and Pakistan*. New York: Columbia University Press, 1980, 91, 236.

pp. 85–86: Mokshodayani Mukhopadhyay, excerpted from "Bangalir Babu" ("The Bengali Babu") in *Banu Pasun*, 1882 (A Bunch of Wild Flowers), trans. Supriya Chaudhury, in *Women Writing in India: 600 B.C. to the Present*, ed. Susie Tharu and K. Lalita. New York: The Feminist Press at The City University of New York, 1991, I:219–21. Translation copyright 1991 by Supriya Chaudhury. English translation reprinted by permission of The Feminist Press at The City University of New York. Compilation copyright 1991 by Susie Tharu and K. Lalita.

pp. 87–88: Letter of Savithribi Phule to Jotiba Phule, October 10, 1856, trans. Maya Pandit, in *Women Writing in India: 600 B.C. to the Present*, ed. Susie Tharu and K. Lalita. New York: The Feminist Press at The City University of New York, 1991, I:213–14. Translation copyright 1991 by Maya Pandit. English translation reprinted by permission of The Feminist Press at The City University of New York. Compilation copyright 1991 by Susie Tharu and K. Lalita.

p. 89: Anti-Footbinding Society of Hunan, "Rules and Regulations on Marriage," in *Chinese Civilization and Society: A Sourcebook*, ed. Patricia Buckley Ebrey. New York: Free Press, 1981, 245–46. Reprinted with the permission of The Free Press, a Division of Simon & Schuster, Inc. Copyright © 1981 by The Free Press.

pp. 90–91: Quoted in Luise White, *The Comforts of Home. Prostitution in Colonial Nairobi*. Chicago: University of Chicago Press, 1990, 55–56, 57, 62–63. Copyright © University of Chicago Press, 1990.

p. 91: Kopinen, 659, quoting Ludwig Kohl-Larsen, ed. *Simbo Janira. Kleiner grosser schwarzer Mann, Lebenserinnerungen eines Buschnegers*. Kassel: Eisenach, 1956.

pp. 96–97: Arthur de Gobineau, *The Inequality of Human Races*. Trans. Adrian Collins. New York: Putnam, 1915, 205–10.

p. 98: *The Works of John Ruskin*. Ed. E. T. Cook and Alexander Wedderburn. 27 vols. London: George Allen, 1905, 16:306–7.

pp. 99–100: *Letters from the Kaiser to the Court*. Ed. Isaac Don Levine. New York: Stokes, 1920, 9–10, 13, 16–17.

pp. 100–1: Uchida Kakichi, Director of Civil Administration. In E. Patricia Tsurumi, *Japanese Colonial Education in Taiwan, 1895–1945*. Cambridge, Mass.: Harvard University Press, 1977, 49.

pp. 100–1: Terauchi Masatake, Governor-general. In Tsurumi, 164.

pp. 101–2: Prince Bariatinskii. Letter to Grand Duke Mikhail Nikolaevich, December 1862. In *Source Book for Russian History from Early Times to 1917*. Ed. George Vernadsky et al. 2 vols. New Haven: Yale University Press, 1972, 2:608–9. Copyright © 1972 Yale University Press.

p. 102–4: From Sumanta Banerjee, "Marginalization of Women's Popular Culture in Nineteenth-Century Bengal." In *Recasting Women in India: Essays in Colonial History*. Ed. Kumkum Sangari and Sudesh Vaid. New Brunswick, N.J.: Rutgers University Press, 1990, 137, 139, 147, 150, 151–52.

pp. 104–5: In Ernest Short, *Fifty Years of Vaudeville*. Westport, Conn.: Greenwood Press, 1978.

pp. 106–7: *New York World*, May 17, May 29, 1896.

pp. 108–9: Claude Debussy, "Taste," in *Debussy on Music*. Ed. and trans. Richard Langham Smith. New York: Knopf, 1977, 278–79.

p. 109: Else Lasker-Schüler, *Your Diamond Dreams Cut Open My Arteries*. Trans. Robert P. Newton. Chapel Hill: University of North Carolina Press, 1982, 137. Copyright © 1983 by the University of North Carolina Press. Used by permission of the publisher.

p. 121: In Blakely, *Blacks in the Dutch World* (1993), 72–73.

pp. 122–23: In Joseph W. Esherick, *The Origins of the Boxer Uprising*. Berkeley: University of California Press, 1987, 299–300. © 1987 Joseph W. Esherick and The Regents of the University of California. Used by permission of the author and the publisher.

pp. 124–25: In Ono Kazuko, *Chinese Women in a Century of Revolution, 1850–1950*. Ed. Joshua Fogel. Stanford, Calif.: Stanford University Press, 1989, 62–63.

pp. 125–26: Hay's circular letter of July 3, 1900. In Henry Steele Commager, *Documents in American History*. 9th ed. 2 vols. Englewood Cliffs, N.J.: Prentice-Hall, 1973, 2:11.

pp. 126–27: Alfred Thayer Mahan, *The Influence of Sea Power Upon History, 1660–1783*. 12th ed. Boston: Little, Brown, 1918, 1, 26, 27, 28.

p. 128: Paul Singer, speech at Social Democratic Party Congress, 1900. In *Germans in the Tropics. Essays in German Colonial History*. Ed. Arthur J. Knoll and Lewis H. Gann. New York: Greenwood, 1987, 61–62.

pp. 129–30: *Rudyard Kipling's Verse, 1885–1918*. Garden City, N.Y.: Doubleday, Page, 1919, 377–78.

p. 130: *Memoirs of Count Witte*. New York: Doubleday, 1921, 186. In *Readings in Russian History*. Ed. Alexander V. Riassanovsky and William H. Watson. Dubuque, Iowa: Kendall/Hunt, 1992, 151.

pp. 130–31: *Memoirs of Baron N. Wrangel, 1847–1920*, trans. Brian and Beatrix Lunn. New York: Lippincott, 1927, 210, 153.

pp. 131–32: Count Shigenobbu Okuma, "The Rise of Japan Was Not Unexpected," in *The Russo-Japanese War Fully Illustrated*, 3 (July 1904): 347–55 passim.

p. 133: Eliezer Tauber, *The Emergence of the Arab Movements*. London: Frank Cass, 1993, 106.

pp. 137–39: Bernhard von Bülow, Speech in the German Reichstag, December 11, 1899. In Ralph R. Menning, *The Art of the Possible. Documents on Great Power Diplomacy 1814–1914*. New York: McGraw-Hill, 1996, 284–85.

pp. 139–40: *Gujarti*. In *India and the War*. Ed. Lord Sydenham of Combe. London: Hodder & Stoughton, 1915, 59–60.

p. 140: Archival material in Marc Michel, *Appel à l'Afrique: Contributions et réactions à l'effort de guerre en A. O. F. (1914–1919)*. Trans. B. G. Smith. Paris: Publications de la Sorbonne, 1982.

p. 141: Patrick Ireland, *Iraq: A Study in Political Development*. New York: Russell & Russell, 1970, 459–60.

pp. 142–43: Covenant of the League of Nations, *The Aims and Organisation of the League of Nations*. Geneva: Secretariat of the League of Nations, 1929, 88.

p. 144: Charles Cros, *La parole est à M. Blaise Diagne, premier homme d'Etat africain*. Paris: self-published, 20–21.

pp. 144–45: Léopold Sédar Senghor, "To the Senegalese Sharpshooters, Dead for France" (1938). In *Black Poets in French*. Ed. Marie Collins. New York: Scribner's, 1972, 111–15.

pp. 149–50: "Report of 25 August 1919." In Alfred Draper, *Amritsar. The Massacre That Ended the Raj*. London: Cassell, 1981, 155.

p. 151: Mohandas K. Gandhi, "My Loincloth," *Hindu*, October 15, 1921. In *Gandhi in India in His Own Words*. Ed. Martin Green. Hanover, N.H.: University Press of New England, 1987, 18–19.

pp. 152–53: *African World*. Supplement, September 1921, xv–xvi, in J. Ayodele Langley, *Pan-Africanism and Nationalism in West Africa, 1900–1945*. Oxford, England: Clarendon, 1973, 76–77.

p. 154: Brenda Bozzoli, *Women of Phokeng: Consciousness, Life Strategy, and Migrancy in South Africa, 1900–1983*. Portsmouth, N.H.: Heinemann, 1991, 162.

p. 155: In Harry Gailey, *The Road to Aba: A Study of British Administrative Policy in Eastern Nigeria*. New York: New York University Press, 1970, 127–28, 133.

p. 156: Badr al-Muluk Bamdad. *From Darkness into Light: Women's Emancipation in Iran*. Hicksville, N.Y.: Exposition Press, 1977, 25–26.

pp. 157–59: Dr. T. Nakayama, *Acupuncture et médecine chinoises vérifiées au Japon*. Trans. T. Sakurazawa and G. Soulié de Morant. Paris: Hippocrate, 1934, 11, 13–14, 46, 61–62. Trans. B. G. Smith.

pp. 160–61: *Ho Chi Minh on Revolution: Selected Writings, 1920–1966*. Ed. Bernard B. Fall. New York: Praeger, 1967, 127–29.

pp. 161–62: Ministry of Education, *Fundamentals of Our National Polity* (1937). In *Sources of Japanese Tradition*. Ed. Ryusaku Tsunoda, William Theodore de Bary, and Donald Keene. New York: Columbia University Press, 1958, 786–87.

pp. 162–63: Hashimoto Kingoro, *The Need for Emigration and Expansion*. International Military Tribunal for the Far East, International Prosecution Section, Document 487B, Exhibit 1290, in *Sources of Japanese Tradition*, 796–98.

p. 163: Tokutomi Iichiro, *The Imperial Rescript Declaring War on the United States and British Empire*, in *Sources of Japanese Tradition*, 800–801.

Sidebars

p. 15: Quoted in Yong Yap and Arthur Cotterell, *Chinese Civilization. From the Ming Revival to Chairman Mao*. London: Weidenfeld and Nicolson, 1977, 102.

p. 19: Quoted in Dun J. Li, *China in Transition 1517–1911*. New York: Van Nostrand Reinhold Co., 1969, 29.

p. 21: Philip Miller, letter of January 12, 1758, quoted in Hazel Le Rougetel, *The Chelsea Gardener: Philip Miller 1691–1771*. Portland: Sagapress, 1990, 86.

p. 31: James Monroe, "The Monroe Doctrine," December 2, 1823.

p. 49: Quoted in Kenneth Pyle, *The New Generation of Meiji Japan: Problems of Cultural Identity, 1885–1895*. Stanford: Stanford University Press, 1969, 159.

p. 78: Carl Akeley quoted in Donna Haraway, *Primate Visions. Gender, Race and Nature in the World of Modern Science*. New York: Routledge, 1989, 53.

p. 88: Letter of Shu-hsien to her sister, 5th day, fourth month, 1903, in *Chinese Civilization and Society: A Sourcebook*. Ed. Patricia Buckley Ebrey. New York: The Free Press, 1981, 246–47.

p. 97: Charles Darwin. *The Descent of Man, and Selection in Relation to Sex*. London: J. Murray, 1871.

p. 101: Quoted in Hans W. Debrunner, *A Church Between Colonial Powers: A Study of the Church in Togo*. Trans. Dorothea M. Barton. London: Lutterworth Press, 1965, 114–15.

p. 104: Quoted in Daniel R. Headrick, *The Tools of Empire. Technology and European Imperialism in the Nineteenth Century*. New York: Oxford University Press, 1981, 116.

p. 131: *Sambay*.

p. 149: Quoted in Alfred Draper, *Amritsar: The Massacre that Ended the Raj*. London: Cassell, 1981, 74.

p. 153: Quoted in J. Ayodele Langley, *Pan-Africanism and Nationalism in West Africa 1900–1945*. Oxford: Clarendon Press, 1973, 73.

Picture Credits

AKG London Ltd.: 143; The Alkazi Collection of Photography: 79 (Raja Deen Dayal & Sons, The Viceroy Lord and Lady Curzon with second day's Trophy during a shikar with the Nizam of Hyderabad [neg. #18852] 1902, gelatin silver print, No. 44/60), 81 (Raja Deen Dayal & Sons, The Viceroy Lord and Lady Curzon on an elephant during a shikar with the Nizam of Hyderabad [neg. #18338] 1902, gelatin silver print, No. 47/60), 112 (Raja Deen Dayal & Sons, At the Gallery to view the Lungar, Moti Bungalow, Visit with the Nizam of Hyderabad [neg. #18377], 1902, gelatin silver print, No. 11/60), 113 (Raja Lala Deen Dayal, A Formal Dinner, Hyderabad [neg. #9608], Sir Asman Jah Album, c. 1890, albumen print. No. 11/75); Courtesy Department of Library Services, American Museum of Natural History/Neg. No. 2A22188, Photo by J. Beckett copy: 97; Archive Photos/Popperfoto: 32, 139; Barnarby's Picture Library: 120; © Bettmann/CORBIS: 128, 145; Bishop Museum, Honolulu, Hawai'i: 51; British Architectural Library, RIBA, London: 44; The British Library, London: 63 (Oriental and India Office Collections), 65, 69; Brown Brothers: 88; Country Life Picture Library: 112; Hawai'i State Archives, Honolulu, Kahn Collection: 53; Hulton Getty/Liaison Agency: 118; The Trustees of the Imperial War Museum, London, neg. no. Q67814: cover, 134; Courtesy of the John Carter Brown Library at Brown University: 31; Katong Antique House, Singapore: 130, 167; Library of Congress: 22 (LC-USZ62-91788), 30 (LC-USZ62-102147), 37 (LC UZ62-106914), 56 (LC-USZ62-99650); 58 (LC-USZ62-102389), 59 (LC-USZ62-103642), 61 (LC-USZ62-10364), 67 (LC-USZ62-93985), 70 (LC-USZ62-99879), 74 (LC-USZ62-46884), 76 (LC-USZ62-107644), 80 (LC-USZ62-214097), 84 (LC-USZ62-96493), 89 (LC-USZC4-1788), 91 (LC-USZ62-122791), 98 (LC-USZ62-108674), 99 (LC USZ62 112657 211065), 101 (LC-USZ62-103630), 108, 113, 116, 127 (LC-USZ62-94098), 129 (LC-USZ62-93904), 138, 142 (LC-USZ62-109572), 146 (LC-USZ62-116140), 155 (Institute of Intercultural Studies), 157 (LC-USZ62-93243), 159 (LC-USZ62-102961), 165 (LC-USZ62-96939), 166 (LC-USZ62-96493); Courtesy of Macclesfield Museums Trust: 25; Manchester City Art Galleries: 18; Mary Evans Picture Library: 92; All Rights Reserved, The Metropolitan Museum of Art: 12; Municipal Archives Haags Gemeenktarchief: 95; Musée d'Histoire Contemporaine: 2; Photo by Irving Solero, Courtesy of the Museum at the Fashion Institute of Technology, New York: 133, 167; Zoe Oliver Sherman Collection, 1922. Courtesy, Museum of Fine Arts, Boston. Reproduced with permission. © 2000 Museum of Fine Arts, Boston. All Rights Reserved: 110; Museum of Modern Art Film Stills Archive: 154; National Archives: 123, 136; By courtesy of the National Portrait Gallery, London: 9, 38, 64; The New York Public Library, Astor, Lenox and Tilden Foundations: 11 (Map Division), 16 (*Chocolate: An Illustrated History*, Maria and Frederic Morton, Science and Business Division), 36 (*The Cambridge Encyclopedia of China*, ed. Brian Hook, General Research Division), 40 (*Holland and Hozier's Record of the Expedition to Abyssinia*, GRD), 83 (GRD), 100 (*South-East Asia, 1930–1970, The Legacy of Colonialism and Nationalism*, Fred R. von der Mehden, GRD), 107 (GRD), 116 (*The Meeting of Eastern and Western Art*, Michael Sullivan, GRD, courtesy of Mr. and Mrs. Peter Quennell, London), 126 (GRD), 151 (*History of Africa*, Kevin Shillington, GRD); Courtesy of Norwich Museum Collection: 82; Courtesy Peabody Essex Museum, Salem, Mass.: 24; Photographie Giraudon/Art Resource, NY: 27; Press Association Photos: 115; Reproduced with permission from *The French in Love and War*, by Charles Rearick (Yale 1997): 157; Rijksmuseum voor Volkenkunde, Leiden/Ben Grishaaver: 158; Robert Opie Collection: 54; Royal Geographical Society, London: 26, 160; Royal Museum of Central Africa–Tervuren: 94; Photographs and Prints Division, Schomburg Center for Research in Black Culture, The New York Public Library, Astor, Lenox and Tilden Foundations: 5, 117 (*The Savage Hits Back*, Julius Lips), 20 (*A Narrative of Four Journeys into the Country of the Hottentots and Caffraria*, William Paterson), 41; Sears, Roebuck & Co.: 132; Courtesy Shiseido Corporate Museum: 114; Courtesy of the Freer Gallery of Art, Smithsonian Institution, Washington, D.C., SC-GR-249: 3; Sunday Telegraph: 137; Tate Gallery, London/Art Resource, NY: 117; Mansell Collection/TIME INC.: 114, 115; Ullstein Bilderdienst, Berlin. 162; Courtesy of the U.S. Bureau of Engraving and Printing: 57; Victoria and Albert Picture Library: 14, 166; Weidenfeld and Nicolson Archives: 9, 103; Wellcome Library, London: 105; Yale Center for British Art, Paul Mellon Collection: 23; Yokohama Archives of History: 48, 131.

Index

Acknowledgments

Many thanks to Carolyn Brown, Joel Kupperman, Patrick McDevitt, and Julie Taddeo for their important contributions, with special appreciation to Todd Shepard for his research assistance and to Marlene Importico for help in preparing the manuscript. Nancy Toff and Karen Fein of Oxford University Press worked skillfully and cheerfully to produce the finished book. Thank you to them for their inspired ideas.

About the Author

Bonnie G. Smith is a professor of history at Rutgers University. She has edited a series for teachers on Women's and Gender History in Global Perspective for the American Historical Association and has served as chair of the test development committee for the Advanced Placement examination in European history. She is the author of books on European, comparative, and women's history, and co-author of *The Making of the West: Peoples and Cultures.*

ML

12/02